UNVEILED IDENTITY

FROM INSIGNIFICANCE TO EMBRACING
YOUR ROYAL IDENTITY IN CHRIST

DEBORAH L. RODRIGUEZ

Disclaimer

This work of nonfiction features the author's personal story in experiencing God's pursuing love in a very profound way. It is based on the author's personal memories and perspective. While every effort has been made to preserve the factual and emotional integrity of these experiences, others involved may remember events differently. To protect the privacy of others mentioned in the story, some names, and identifying details have been left out.

GET YOUR FREE GIFT!

We are giving you decorative Scripture reference pages titled, "God says I am…" that will guide you towards gaining greater clarity into who God calls you.

Download your free gift by visiting:
bit.ly/4nnHqzN

Or scan this QR Code

DEDICATION

To you, precious one, who has yet to experience God our Creator as the God who delights in you, who is ever mindful of you, who knows your name, and who has engraved it on the palm of His hands.

(Isaiah 49:16)

.

CONTENTS

FOREWARD

*I*n *Unveiled Identity,* Deborah has beautifully shared her journey of struggling with a sense of insignificance and unworthiness to freedom and joy through an unveiling of seeing herself as God sees her in her true identity as a royal child of God. She weaves her own experiences in with encouraging and insightful scripture, and the *Key Takeaways* and *Let's Reflect* questions at the end of each chapter are very helpful in personally going deeper with God and asking Him to "unveil" His truth to you in each area of chapter focus.

Unveiled Identity is a great encouragement and reminder of how much our amazing Heavenly Father lavishly loves us, sees us as His own, and desires for us to live fully in our royal identity in Him!

Jennifer Brommet
Founder/Director True Identity Ministries
Author of *True Identity*
jbrommet@trueidentityministries.org
www.TrueIdentityMinistries.org

Raised in an unhealthy atmosphere that left me feeling less than, I found it hard to believe I would ever know love and hid many secret truths behind veils of insecurity and drama. As a young adult, I found Christ through reading the Bible and realized Christ's sacrificial death was personal. Studying the names of God and the stories of people God interacted with, unveiled God's identity to me – showing all He is, how He loves me unconditionally, and how He wants me to have a personal relationship with Him.

Whether you know about Christ, or whether you already know Him, I have every confidence that journeying through Deborah's walk with God will draw you closer to Him, open your heart to unveil yourself to Him, and live in victorious expectation of all He has for you.

Delores Liesner
Author of *Be the Miracle* – 31 true stories of faith in action
Writings published in *Chicken Soup for the Soul, Focus on the Family and Guidepost* books.
http://www.deloresliesner.com
Deloresbethemiracle@gmail.com

HOW TO USE THIS BOOK

Welcome to a journey of discovery!

*A*s my journey unfolds, from insignificance to embracing my royal identity in Christ, one chapter builds on another. So don't skip any chapters! Scripture and reflection questions are provided to help you break through a poverty mentality to one of Biblical abundance. You are encouraged to pen your thoughts in a notebook or journal in answer to reflection questions.

Growing from feelings of insignificance to embracing your royal identity in Christ is a journey that is even richer with a friend or a group for accountability and support. You can:

1. Read the chapter in advance and answer the reflection questions before you meet to discuss them. Pray with one another.
2. Read the chapter in advance, then answer and discuss reflection questions at the time you meet with each other. Pray with one another.
3. At the end of each chapter, you'll find a hymn to lift your heart in worship. You can scan the QR code to sing along as my sister, Ruth Hartunian-Alumbaugh, beautifully accompanies on piano, or visit my website

and click "Hymns in My Book" at the bottom right of the page.

authordeborahrodriguez.com

God's Word revealed a gold mine that transformed my life. Read on to see how He wants to do the same for you!

INTRODUCTION

*I*nsignificant. Undeserving. Unworthy. Do these words define you? Positive recognition can be perceived as unjustified. Receiving a gift can be difficult when we internally reject it with thoughts of undue attention. A reward is mentally identified as something someone else warrants, not ourselves. We belittle ourselves for the sake of humility. Imagine interpreting Scripture such as, *"Let nothing be done through selfish ambition or conceit, but in lowliness of mind let each esteem others better than himself"* (Philippians 2:3-4), as: "I am not important; you are important," or, "My feelings don't matter; your feelings do matter." This was me.

I didn't know these thoughts and feelings led me to squelch the words "I" and "me." Why was this me? How did this happen? Eagerly seeking answers, I discovered it was more of a quest, not so much my own, but of God's love pursuing me. Just as a pendulum swings from one extreme to another, then eventually arrives at the central point of equilibrium, God revealed the truths I believed in God's Word that were out of balance. He unveiled enslaving beliefs that cheated me of God-given value.

Who would have ever thought my identity and worth were greatly lacking? I was involved in ministry opportunities and positions for over 35 years, a pastor's wife of a very special church for 25 years, a home-educator of six children for 26 years, a registered nurse on sabbatical caring for our youngest daughter (who had nine surgeries in nine years), and a caregiver for my cherished aging parents. My life was about meeting needs wherever I turned. Living the dream of doing all my favorite things, I believed I could "do all things through Christ who strengthens me." I was too busy to notice...

Until one day, God's love broke through like a dam unleashed and unveiled my priceless worth.

Unveiled Identity is written for those of us who crave to venture from the struggle of insignificance to an unveiling of who we are in Christ, from devaluing yourself to experiencing transformation in seeing yourself through God's eyes. It's for those who have left the ingredient out of your walk with God that reconstructs and revolutionizes your thinking to see yourself as a royal child of the King of Kings, Jesus Christ. Are His rewards and blessings difficult or even burdensome for you to accept? Then *Unveiled Identity* is for you.

What would it take for you to experience the significance of who you were created to be? God calls you His special treasure. Redeemed. Forgiven. More than a conqueror. Overcomer. Confident. Rejoiced over. Victorious. Loved. Rescued. Fearfully and wonderfully made. Royalty. Because what God says is true, I can promise you that as you allow God to reveal who He truly is and embrace His definition of your true identity, you will inevitably experience an intimacy with Jesus Christ you never knew. And don't be surprised when your confidence in Him gives you confidence in how you see yourself.

Come with me on a journey that includes a "custom made storm" allowed by the Creator. Your journey may not look like mine, but my hope and prayer for you is to have an unveiling of truth out of balance and for you to believe you can be that person who walks with assurance in your identity in Christ Jesus. Be at peace and quietly rest, knowing that He delights in His children as we abide in Him.

Don't delay your journey any longer. Turn the page to begin a life-changing transformation now!

IDENTITY AWAKENED

She was a friend in the truest sense, like "iron sharpening iron," yet full of grace. With eyes that seemed to search mine, as if to communicate to my heart, she gently revealed a part of me that I was oblivious to. I handed her a rough draft of a letter I wrote and asked her if the words reflected my heart to my loved one. "You said 'she' instead of 'I' and 'her' instead of 'me,'" she declared gently. Perceiving this to be normal, I made nothing of it. But finally, patiently, she broke through. She revealed that I couldn't articulate the words "me" or "I" in my message. Instead, I had written in the third person, using "she" or "her" every time I referred to myself. This revelation left me bewildered and almost paralyzed, yet her statement motivated me to prayerfully investigate why it was so.

My life was filled with the joys and challenges of mothering six children, the blessings and unfamiliar encounters as a new pastor's wife, and the unchartered learning curve and fulfillment of all that home education involves. Accompanying that was the privilege of caring for my elderly parents, and the concentrated care of our youngest daughter through nine surgeries, countless physical therapy appointments, and more. I was unaware that giving and serving others needed the balance of stewarding my own life as well. How did I come to this awakening? Let me take you on a journey.

Over the course of time, three friends at three different times caringly suggested I read the book *Boundaries* by Dr. Henry Cloud and Dr. John Townsend. After I read the book, one idea that resonated with me was that, as innocent as I may be, I may have read God's Word with my own perceptions or sat under teaching that has misled me in my understanding of boundaries. I was awakened to the fact that I didn't have healthy boundaries in the area of service, or more importantly, in the area of personal stewardship.

So, what is a boundary? Simply put, "Boundaries are personal property lines that define who you are and who you are not, and influence all areas of your life."[1] Why are boundaries there? Because they send a message that says, "My property ends here, and your property begins there." "This is my responsibility, and this is your responsibility." "I own this, and you own that." I don't expect you to be responsible for caring for my property; neither should you expect me to be responsible for taking care of yours.[2] For example, if I am exhausted from caring for others' needs, it's okay to responsibly take a nap to refresh myself to be able to give of my best, not only physically, but also mentally and emotionally. Another example is, when I identify with a need someone has, I need to discern if I am the one to fill the need or if God or someone else should be the one to fill that need.

Sometimes we just don't know how unhealthy our boundaries are until we experience healthy ones. It's like unwittingly living your whole life with a thyroid hormone imbalance, then through testing, finally finding out this is why you have been so weary. You then start taking supplements

---

[1] Henry Cloud and John Townsend, *Boundaries* (Grand Rapids, MI: Zondervan, 2004), inside cover.
[2] Ibid., 29.

or medication to accommodate the imbalance. Amazing! Energy now abounds! This was the case for me, spiritually and emotionally. I was unaware that I had an imbalance in my understanding of stewardship versus selfishness.

My mind was whirling with revelation! I learned that it is not selfish to steward your life well. What is stewardship? According to Merriam Webster, stewardship is "the conducting, supervising, or managing of something, *especially:* the careful and responsible management of something entrusted to one's care."[3] Although the application of stewardship is usually in the form of investments, estates, or natural resources, we can apply the definition to our lives. We can manage our life carefully and responsibly without feeling selfish because God has entrusted it to our care! This includes our body, spirit, and soul (mind, will, emotions). God has entrusted to us a life of eternal value. *"Or do you not know that your body is the temple of the Holy spirit who is in you, whom you have from God, and you are not your own? For you were bought at a price, Therefore glorify God in your body and in your spirit, which are God's"* (I Corinthians 6:19-20). How are we stewarding that life?

Here are a few questions to consider. Do you, like I did, find it easy to see a need and take the responsibility to fill it? Are you keenly aware of the feelings going on around you and do you try to satisfy peoples' every "need" so that they can feel better? Is serving something that brings you joy? "Isn't this what Christ did?" you may exclaim. Yes! These are all good character traits; however, not at the expense of your very soul withering away.

---

[3] "Stewardship," *Merriam-Webster.com*, 2019, https://www.merriam-webster.com (accessed October 28, 2019).

I compare it to the pre-flight safety briefing we hear before take-off. You know, the part that explains the use of the oxygen mask. The passenger should always fit his or her own mask properly before helping children, the disabled, or any persons requiring assistance. If you aren't saturated with oxygen yourself, you can't very well last long enough to assist someone else to get their own oxygen. I became aware that I ignored the fact that it's okay to look out for my own interests along with the interests of others: *"Let each of you look out not only for **his own** interests, but also for the interests of others"* (Philipians 2:4, emphasis added). Why did I focus only on the interests of others? Why was I not mindful that I had some of my own? God does want us to bless others, but not at the price of destroying or neglecting our own health. I was unaware that giving and serving others needed the balance of stewarding my own life as well. My friend's words brought me unexpectedly to this startling consciousness.

Let's look at the biblical account of the Good Samaritan in Luke 10:30-35 as an object lesson for this truth:

> *"...A certain man went down from Jerusalem to Jericho, and fell among thieves, who stripped him of his clothing, wounded him, and departed, leaving him half dead. A priest and a Levite came down the road, saw him half dead, and passed by on the other side of the road. But a certain Samaritan, as he journeyed, came where he was. And when he saw him, he had compassion. So he went to him and bandaged his wounds, pouring on oil and wine; and he set him on his own animal, brought him to an inn, and took care of him. On the next day when he departed, he took out two denarii, gave them to the innkeeper, and said*

to him, 'Take care of him; and whatever more you spend, when I come again, I will repay you.'"

Townsend and Cloud put a twist on the story here and proclaim, suppose the injured man wakes up at this point in the story and says:

"What? You're leaving?"

"Yes, I am. I have some business in Jericho I have to attend to," the Samaritan replies.

"Don't you think you're being selfish? I'm in pretty bad shape here. I'm going to need someone to talk to. How is Jesus going to use you as an example? You're not even acting like a Christian, abandoning me like this in my time of need! Whatever happened to 'Deny yourself?'"

"Why, I guess you're right," the Samaritan says. "That would be uncaring of me to leave you here alone. I should do more. I will postpone my trip for a few days."

So he stays with the man for three days, talking to him and making sure that he is happy and content. On the afternoon of the third day, there's a knock at the door and a messenger comes in. He hands the Samaritan a message from his business contacts in Jericho: "Waited as long as we could. Have decided to sell camels to another party. Our next herd will be here in six months."

"How could you do this to me?" the Samaritan screams at the recovering man, waving the message in the air. "Look what you've done now! You've caused me to lose those camels that I needed for my *business. Now I can't deliver my goods. This may put me out of business! How could you do this to me?"[4]*

Think about how you would respond to the message from the business contacts in Jericho if you were the good Samaritan—his response above- #1, or #2, #3, or make up your own:

#2 "Oh no! Lord, help! You are my Strength and Provider. You promised me that all things work together for good to those who love You and are called according to Your purpose. You give and take away. Besides, 'I can do all things through Christ who strengthens me.' I trust this to your Almighty hands. Please guide me in what to do."

#3 "Lord, I realize that You called me to be compassionate to those in need, but I see now how I've neglected the business You have blessed me with, and for some reason I've given more than I can give. There is something I lack in my own life to allow this to happen. Show me what that is so that I may be a good steward of who and how You made me. Show me what I am truly responsible for, and to what extent I should carry my burdens."

I was living my life in #2. There appears to be so much truth in that answer, right? I perceived that I had my oxygen mask on, but God was exposing the deception I was believing. I didn't take into consideration the fact that I could be a loving person and set limits at the same time. I was beginning to understand that we need to steward not only our time, talents, money, and possessions but also our love, energy, and mental/emotional health. Every part of our personal life needs to be stewarded well for God's glory, and it isn't selfish to say "no" when the boundary line gets crossed.

---

[4] Cloud and Townsend, *Boundaries*, 38–39.

Awakening to this awareness of my real "self" felt, well, selfish. I rebelled. Yet, I asked God what His truth was. Over time and healing, I came to understand some principles of stewardship. I learned that guilt about stewarding my mind, will, emotions, body, and spirit was false guilt. I gained an understanding that I am not selfish to "manage" my life carefully and responsibly because God has entrusted it to me to care for it. If I am not stewarding "me" well—the "me" God so amazingly fashioned-something in my life will give way or become fractured.

So, are boundaries intended for us to put our focus on ourselves instead of others? No, just the opposite. According to Merriam-Webster, selfish means "concerned excessively or exclusively with oneself; seeking or concentrating on one's own advantage, pleasure, or well-being without regard for others."[5] Selfishness prevents us from loving others the way Christ would. Boundaries enable us to love others more readily and abundantly because we give and serve out of our health... like Jesus.

How do we manage this gift of life? How do we take good care of our health physically, mentally, emotionally, and spiritually? According to I Corinthians 6:19-20 it says, *"Or do you not know that your body is the temple of the Holy Spirit who is in you, whom you have from God, and you are not our own? For you were bought at a price; therefore glorify God in your body and in your spirit, which are God's."* In order to glorify God in my body and spirit, I have to recognize that an absence of boundaries can cause me to mismanage the temple or property God has invested in. God as the Owner has a right to be dissatisfied with me. When we say "no"

---

[5] "Selfish," Merriam-Webster.com, 2019, https://www.merriam-webster.com (accessed October 29, 2019).

to people and activities that will end up hurting us, we are protecting God's investment. Our spiritual and emotional development is God's "interest" on His investment in us.[6] Clearly, there is a difference between selfishness and stewardship.

This analogy of God being the Owner and me being the steward of His investment stirred my inquisitive mind in areas I never thought of. I learned that there were areas I was taking responsibility for that were not my place to take responsibility for and I was not taking responsibility for areas I needed to take responsibility for:

- ✿ Emotions: Although we are not to let feelings rule our lives, we also cannot deny them as if they don't matter. My feelings were brushed aside as I sought to nurture and meet the needs of others. Sharing my feelings was not a practice since I believed it would burden someone to carry them. However, I was very available to carry someone else's burden.

- ✿ Attitudes and Beliefs: Although we are responsible for our own attitudes and beliefs, we cannot take responsibility for those of others. I was really good at taking the blame for other people's attitudes. I felt as though I was the cause of their unhealthy or hurtful words, thoughts, actions, and motives. This view caused me to have a victim mentality.

- ✿ Behavior: We are only responsible for our own behavior, not someone else's. I thought I was "helping" someone with a need when it was a reoccurring need due to their irresponsibility. Assuming the responsibility to rescue someone from irresponsible

---

[6] Cloud and Townsend, *Boundaries*, 105.

behaviors interrupts the law of sowing and reaping and can enable them to continue on their downward spiral of destructive living. I was an enabler.

✿ Choices: Although we are to take responsibility for our personal choices, we also have a voice in the choices we need to make together with others in teamwork, business, friendship, and marriage. I felt I didn't have a voice to communicate my choices and desires, especially if others disagreed with them. I also took the blame or responsibility for their poor choices.

✿ Values: Our values do count even if others do not share them. Our values show what we love and do not love, what we believe or do not believe. I would negate my values if others did not share them. When I deferred to someone else's values which weren't my own I felt guilty, as an accomplice to their negative actions. I was not true to the convictions God gave me.

✿ Mind, will, emotions, and body: We have limits with the capacity of our mind, will, emotions, and body. When I was exhausted, I felt guilty when I rested. If my cognition took me only so far, I felt guilty when reaching out to ask for help, thinking I was a bother. If I discerned something was destroying a relationship, I believed I would be critical if I shared these feelings, even though I wanted to be closer—emotionally, spiritually, mentally, and physically.

✿ Talents and gifts: Our gifts and talents are evidence of God's marvelous workmanship in us. Joy and fulfillment come from operating in the niche God fashioned for us to thrive. I would often negate or ignore the fulfillment they bring because I felt it's self-centered to do so.

✿ Thoughts: We need to take our own thoughts and feelings captive under the obedience of Jesus Christ. Surrendering to the truth of God's Word is our own responsibility; however, we cannot assume that others can read our mind. I felt my thoughts were insignificant compared to someone else's. I often did not share my thoughts.

✿ Desires: We have dreams, desires, and goals that God has created us with since the beginning of time, and He does want us to fulfill them. We are not on this earth to only serve or help in fulfilling others' desires but our own as well. I felt fulfilling my dreams and goals was self-centered and unimportant even if I knew God would be pleased with them.

✿ Love: If I can only give love without feeling worthy of receiving love in return, I will become depleted. In my depletion, I will not be able to love the way Christ would love. I must be replenished. I didn't see myself as significant enough to be worthy of the same love I gave away.

Stewarding our life well includes all of these areas and more. To focus on one or a few areas and negate the others can lead to an unbalanced life.

Awareness of my unhealthy condition was growing very, very slowly—but surely. Serving God was a privilege to resolutely keep my priorities in order: God first, husband second, children third, and ministry outflowing beyond that. I hadn't considered myself in the mix of servanthood. Recognizing the vast chasm between ideas of stewardship I had held up until now and the new areas of stewardship I was learning brought me to a place of inner turmoil. My mind, spirit, and emotions were challenged. God's pursuing love led me to an understanding I hadn't known before. As one peels an onion one layer at a time, so my soul was being dismantled.

Key TakeAways:

✦ Becoming aware of ingrained, misleading thoughts in our lives regarding Biblical truth is the first step to healing.

✦ Physical, mental, emotional, and spiritual boundaries are God-given tools and are needed for a healthy life.

✦ As we look out for the interests of others, we need to remember to embrace who God created us to be and steward our own lives as well.

✦ Stewarding our life—our mind, will, emotions, body, and spirit—is not selfish.

✦ Our life is a gift from God. We must take the responsibility of managing it for our Owner, Jesus Christ.

Let's Reflect:

1. Consider which friends in your life are true friends; those who draw you closer to the Lord. Proverbs 27:17 states, *"As iron sharpens iron, so a man sharpens the countenance of his friend."* God used true friends in my life, who with sensitivity, revealed who I really was instead of silently, complacently allowing me to believe who I thought I was. Do you have a friend like that? If not, prayerfully seek one. Consider yielding to the faithful God, your Creator, who may send His message through true friends because He loves and cares for you.

2. We can manage our personal life carefully and responsibly without feeling selfish because God has entrusted it to our care! Read Philippians 2:4. Ask the Lord to bring to mind the areas where boundaries are unbalanced, especially the areas that are harming you spiritually, mentally, emotionally, and physically. If you need help to get started, look at the bullet points listed in this chapter. Ask God for His grace to bring truth to these areas to set you free. Journal your journey.

3. After taking inventory of boundary breakers, led by the Holy Spirit, present your body (mind, will, emotions, spirit, and physical body) as a living sacrifice to God. *"I beseech you therefore, brethren, by the mercies of God, that you present your bodies a living sacrifice, holy, acceptable to God, which is your reasonable service,"* (Romans 12:1). What He owns, He compels us to take good care of. Write your prayer.

Let's Pray:

Oh, God, Creator of the universe, grant us spiritual eyes to discern how we truly view ourselves and expose what hinders us from knowing who we really are in Christ. Break through every layer of our soul to unveil what caused us to get "lost," and help us find our way back to the truth of the wonderful, marvelous workmanship You created us to be from the beginning. Thank You for loving us so much to reveal this to us in your faithfulness. Lord, *"perfect that which concerns us"* (Psalm 138:8). In Jesus' name, Amen.

Let's Sing:

Sing along with my sister on piano by scanning the QR code or visit my website under "Hymns in My Book."

authordeborahrodriguez.com

IDENTITY CHALLENGED

*W*e are physical, emotional, mental, and spiritual beings. To disregard or underestimate one facet of how God fashioned us will cause a breakdown or imbalance in other areas. To focus on physical health and neglect spiritual health can cause a lack in our well being, even harm. Focusing on spiritual health while neglecting emotional health will bring disharmony and, moreover, self-destruction. My heart was fixed at a young age to love and serve the God who gave His life for me. My roles and callings were clear: wife, mom to six precious blessings, home educator, daughter/caregiver of my aging parents, and fulfilling various ministry opportunities in church/ministry. When my eyes first opened in the morning, I already knew what I was to do—serve gladly.

God continued to challenge truth out of balance. I needed help. In God's pursuing love, He led me to recommended resources written by Peter and Geri Scazzero, a pastor and his wife. Enlightened, I discovered I was taking over-responsibility of the "needs" or perceived feelings of others without being in tune with how God created me with legitimate needs. In the name of claiming the promise, *"I can do all things through Christ who strengthens me"* (Philipians 4:13), I believed I had the strength, grace, and comfort of our Abba Father to face any challenge—including challenges He very possibly didn't want me to face. This captured my attention because in my service to others, I started to question whether I was submitting to Christ or simply to "needs." I was awakened to a few traits I had developed, through no fault of others:

✿ I chose to "do" for others in the name of "helping them" when in reality they could/should have done it themselves.

✿ In my desire to use God-given talents to the best of my ability, I was quick to instruct others or "fix" a situation to prevent it from becoming problematic. It wasn't always my responsibility to take this role.

✿ I took uninvited liberty to help others solve problems instead of exercising discernment and asking the Lord if I need to allow that person to grow through their struggle so they could learn how to hear from God and grow in faith through their trials.

✿ I was a "yes" person, without counting the cost of how it would affect me or what was already going on in my life.

✿ I concealed the shortcomings of others at my own expense or "rescued" them with consequences to my own health.

✿ I loved to help people, but often did not ask for help because I didn't want to burden others.

I was over-functioning at the price of blindly neglecting myself. Does this sound familiar in your life? For example, Jesus understands our desire to lovingly serve Him, yet He intends for us to take responsibility for our own needs. Refreshing ourselves by visiting a close friend, seeking wisdom from godly counsel, or clearing our schedule to have time to regroup can rejuvenate us so we can freely serve from abundance. Not depletion. Stewarding our lives well also includes knowing the limits with which God Himself created us.

Expressing our thoughts and feelings verbally is key to understanding one another. Voicing thoughts and feelings honestly may be easy for some, but in the name of denying ourselves and picking up our cross daily (Matthew 16:24), one may stuff those thoughts and feelings inside. "Failing to acknowledge what is going on in your heart eventually results in losing connection with yourself. And if you lose connection with yourself, you easily slip out of dependency on God's Spirit. Spiritual growth and loving well then become virtually impossible."[7]

Caring for a sick or hospitalized child, preparing the next lesson for our children's school day, or taking on more than I should when I saw my husband spinning too many plates in the ministry brought me joy and fulfillment (most of the time). However, I often took no thought of voicing that I had the need for rest—even Sabbath rest. Rest became even less possible after hearing some unsettling news from the pediatric geneticist. He announced that our 4-year-old possibly had osteogenesis imperfecta, a type of rare brittle bone disease that affects how the body makes collagen. Bone fractures can be easily acquired by little pressure. My mind was in a whirlwind. The year before this, she had had two major surgeries to correct a congenital dysplasia of her right femur, putting her in a body cast for six weeks after the first surgery and eleven weeks after the second. In the past year, she had broken her femur and tibia. Now she needed to be closely supervised to prevent any

---

[7] Geri Scazzero and Peter Scazzero, *The Emotionally Healthy Woman* (Grand Rapids, MI: Zondervan, 2013), 77.

more occurrences of fractured bones. I informed the family of this new way of living. A set of eyes needed to be watching her every minute of every day, and one of us needed to grip her hand everywhere she went.

The next day, all five children were enthusiastically hitting balloons into the air and our 4-year-old wanted to join in. Of course I couldn't say no to this fun, so I held her hand wherever she jumped to punch the balloon. After about 45 minutes of this animated activity, I slumped to the couch with her in my arms, drained and exhausted.

My heavy, reluctant heart gave way to a surrendered, committed heart which placed her in the tender care of our Great Protector, the Lord Jesus Christ. We no longer held her hand everywhere she went but continued to keep a close watch over her. It was such a release, emotionally and mentally, to entrust her to the One who had the greater ability to be everywhere all the time and who loved her even more than her family could. Eventually, we were told by our daughter's pediatric orthopedic surgeon that she didn't have the rare disease after all. What a relief!

Also around this time, I had the heart-rending, yet joyous privilege of caring for my loving mom in our home in the last hours of her life. Besides being my best friend and the most influential woman in my life, she was my cheerleader for the principles I was learning. I felt such a great loss from her absence after her home-going that I felt like I needed an anchor—someone to "pull me in" occasionally if I strayed a bit from where I was supposed to be.

I began praying for a mentor. I needed someone to be that godly sounding board who pointed me to the true answer to everything—Jesus Christ and His Word. After a few months of prayer, I picked up the phone to call a friend who I was sure was the mentor God had for me. As it turned out, I couldn't tell who was more blessed, she or I! With wisdom and compassion, my 85-year-old friend encouraged me in what I had learned about stewarding my life and patiently helped me flesh out what that meant practically in day-to-day life. In a sense, God in flesh came to me and provided what I needed through her.

God's pursuing love addressed the truth that I was out of balance in my life. In time, God would reveal a heart that needed to be refashioned in the days and months ahead.

Key Take-aways:

- ✦ We are physical, emotional, mental, and spiritual beings. To neglect any one facet of how God fashioned us may cause a breakdown in other areas.
- ✦ Be aware to ensure we submit to Christ and not the perceived "needs" of those we serve.
- ✦ It's okay to voice our thoughts and feelings honestly and respectfully without feeling like we are a burden.
- ✦ Stewarding our lives well also includes knowing the limits with which God Himself created us to have.
- ✦ Entrusting our cares to the tender heart of God brings rest.

Let's Reflect:

1. Contemplate what you do with your time and why you do it. You are a human *being*, not a human *doing*. Ask God to rearrange your priorities to include refreshing and reviving your spirit, soul, and body so that you can give your best to the Master. What is He saying to you? Remember to *"Be still, and know that I am God"* (Psalm 46:10) as you seek His answer.

2. Audibly proclaim, *"I will praise You (God), for I am fearfully and wonderfully made; marvelous are Your works, and that my soul knows very well"* (Psalm 139:14). Express it as a response to God who is conveying to you how intricately He fashioned you in His image. Meditate on this verse and imagine how marvelous you are to God. Count the ways He has made you masterfully unique with your talents, giftings, cognitive abilities, and even your limitations. Make a list.

3. As truth is challenged in who you are in Christ, you will find that you can't be on this journey alone. We were uniquely fashioned with a need for relationship and fellowship since the Garden of Eden. Begin praying for a mentor to keep you accountable to the truth you are discovering. Make sure they are godly and point you to the Answer, Jesus Christ, and not their own opinions. Write your prayer.

Let's Pray:

We thank You, Lord, that You have fearfully and wonderfully made us. We are Your workmanship created to do Your good works, and You have crafted us with Your own loving hand.

Remind us over and over again of this. You are our resting place. We can trust in You as we place who You made us to be, in Your mighty hands. In Jesus' Name, Amen.

Let's Sing:

Sing along with my sister on piano by scanning the QR code or visit my website under "Hymns in My Book."

authordeborahrodriguez.com

IDENTITY REVEALED

*A*fter awakening to *what* was lacking in my life, I began to search for *why*. Truth began to expose perceptions and deceptions. Perceptions can be almost "mystical." While visiting my sister, Ruth, in Connecticut, my mouth was literally gaping as I heard her recount some of our childhood memories. As we reminisced, she gave accounts of family events we attended that didn't turn out so well, yet my description of those events didn't include any of the negative aspects she was describing. I was astounded! Finally, I burst out, "Was I even there?!"

This experience was significant because as I was reclaiming my identity, I was discovering that I had perceptions of what God said that were inaccurate. Of course, a perception cannot really be inaccurate, right? Perceptions are personal observations, discernment, experiences, and opinions. However, the perceptions I was living out were based on verses such as:

✿ *"...if anyone desires to come after Me, let him deny himself, and take up his cross, and follow Me"* (Matthew 16:24).

✿ *"Let nothing be done through selfish ambition or conceit, but in lowliness of mind let each esteem others better than himself"* (Philippians 2:3-4).

- ✣ *"Greater love has no one than this, than to lay down one's life for his friends"* (John 15:13).

- ✣ *"'And you shall love the Lord your God with all your heart, with all your soul, with all your mind, and with all your strength.' This is the first commandment. And the second, like it, is this: 'You shall love your neighbor as yourself.' There is no other commandment greater than these"* (Mark 12:30-31).

God revealed to me that the conclusion I formed from these verses was, "I am nothing, you are everything." "I am not important; you are important." "My feelings don't matter; your feelings do matter." "My interests are not to be valued; your interests are to be valued." "I will give and give (lay down my life), but I'm not worth you giving to me."

The revelation of all revelations as I read these Scriptures again was that I was to love my neighbor *as myself*! As myself? Ouch! That sounded downright self-centered! The order here was revealed as never before: First, love God. Second, love your neighbor and love yourself equally—love your neighbor *as* yourself. I was awestruck!

Let me put this verse in perspective for you. Imagine, for a moment, a few scenarios. One may bring a smile to your face, one may make you angry. One may even sound ludicrous. Visualize an orthodontist with crooked teeth while he is meticulously evaluating the x-ray to professionally align your teeth for a nice smile. Envision a car mechanic fixing everyone else's car to ensure its safety, but his car hasn't been on a maintenance schedule since he bought it. Picture a nurse who ignores her own disease and symptoms but brings healing and restoration to her patient. Picture a carpenter who constructs magnificent mansions, but his own house is deteriorating. Imagine a personal coach at the fitness center overweight, eating potato chips as you arrive for your first training session. It appears as though one is valuing the receiver of the service, but not valuing oneself. The value you see in others needs to be embraced as value that you have as well.

Did I value myself like I value my neighbor? Did I treat myself like I treat my neighbor? Could I ask for a cup of tea when I'm sick without feeling like a burden, just as I would bring a cup of tea for you? Just as I would love to bless a family with a home-cooked meal after bringing their newborn home from the hospital, could I receive a meal from you without feeling like I'm not worth the trouble? Did I value myself as Christ values me? What did this all mean? Over time and healing, I discovered that in order to really love my neighbor as Christ did, I needed to love what Christ loves... and that included me. I cannot give away what I do not possess. I cannot give love in its fullest sense unless I receive it myself.

The revelation of truth can be unsettling, yet freeing. As these truths out of balance were revealed, the Biblical passage came to mind when Satan tempted Jesus using Scripture to try to cause the Son of God to stumble. How downright appalling! Do you remember the account? At one point, Satan and Jesus are on the pinnacle of the temple in the Holy City. Satan sneers, *"If You are the Son of God, throw Yourself down. For it is written: 'He shall give His angels charge over you,' and 'In their hands they shall bear you up, lest you dash your foot against a stone.'"* Jesus' answer was, *"It is written again, 'You shall not tempt the LORD your God'"* (Matthew 4:6-7). Just as Satan twisted Scripture out of balance to get Jesus to sin, I too had believed a truth, but it was unbelievably out of balance.

In God's faithfulness, He continued to reveal the truth about my identity, which was fixed and redeemed at the cross. While conversing about our Sunday School lesson with a friend one Sunday afternoon, I said emphatically, "I could never ask God for a reward. He has blessed me with so much already!" God's smile on my life as I walked with Him sufficed... until my friend reminded me of the balancing truth: "Jabez asked God to bless him. Besides, there are Scriptures that tell of how God rewards His children."

My heart was undeniably pricked by my Gentle Shepherd as this truth was revealed. As I stood there, pondering blessings and rewards, the next words that came out of my mouth, prompted by Scripture, caused me to become undone: "Someday we will cast our crowns before His feet." I knew that as God's children, we will be given a crown of life when we see Him face to face. My mind went to Revelation 4:10-11, "...the twenty-four elders fall down before Him who sits on the throne and worship Him who lives forever and ever, and cast their crowns before the throne, saying: 'You are worthy, O Lord, To receive glory and honor and power; For You created all things, And by Your will they exist and were created.'" Granted, this Scripture describes the 24 elders casting their crowns before Christ's feet, but I wondered if we, too, out of utter awe and worship, will cast our crown(s) before His feet. If so, that meant I would need to receive a crown to cast! I was absolutely riveted. I imagined myself bowing prostrate before the throne of the One who loves me so. As God's unworthy child, I was wearing a brilliant, gleaming crown, which I had done nothing to attain in my own strength. Understanding that I will give Him only what He has enabled me to possess, I cast that crown at His more-than-worthy feet out of reverence, awe, and love. I envisioned casting not one, but many crowns before His feet out of profound gratitude because He is infinitely worthy!

Humbled and awestruck as a result of this truth, I wanted to know how I could become one who was seeking that blessing like Jabez, and know what that reward truly was, so I could cast many crowns at His loving, priceless, deserving, nail-scarred feet someday. My worth, and my unworthiness of His blessings and rewards, were inconceivable.

In my eagerness and longing, I wanted to learn how God took an insignificant person and called him blessed—even royalty. He can do the same for you, just as He did for me.

Key Take-Aways:

+ It is vital to be aware of our perceptions about God and His Word. Wrong perceptions could lead to truth out of balance.
+ Jesus said to love your neighbor *as yourself*.
+ In order to really love our neighbor as Christ did, we need to love and value what Christ loves and values... and that includes ourselves. Yes, He values you too! I cannot give away what I do not possess.
+ I cannot give love in its fullest sense unless I receive it myself.
+ Jabez asked God to bless him. We can too.
+ We will one day cast our crowns before the nail-scarred feet of our Sovereign Lord and Savior, Jesus Christ, who enables us to possess those crowns in the first place.

Let's Reflect:

1. Identify perceptions in your life. That may be hard to do by yourself because your perceptions are a part of who you are. Maybe you have a loved one, a Bible verse, or even a life circumstance that God is using to get your attention in order for you to see things differently, understand yourself more clearly, to know and experience Him more profoundly, and to trust God's Word purposefully. What could that be? Often, God will get our attention through unhealthy or unbalanced patterns we have in our life. Seek Him. Ask Him. Read Jeremiah 17:10 and Psalm 139:23-24. Pen your thoughts.

2. Ponder how you see yourself. Are rewards difficult for you to accept? Why? Where does this belief or attitude come from? Proverbs 23:7 says, *"As [a man] thinks in his heart, so is he."* Do you self-talk? Do you say things like, "I'm not important." "I'm a loser." "I'm ugly." "I'm a failure." "I don't think I'm worth the trouble." "I'm dumb." Understandably, we have faults in our life that we need to confess to God and others. We will always have things to grow in or to change. However, how we think about ourselves in our heart becomes who we are. Renew your mind with who God says you are: *"For you are a holy people to the LORD your God, and the LORD has chosen you to be a people for Himself, a special treasure above all the peoples who are on the face of the earth"* (Deuteronomy 14:2). Did you catch that? You are a special treasure! Search for any other Biblical references of names and titles of who God calls you to be (See Appendix E for ideas). Record the ones that resonate with you.

3. In Revelation 4:10-11, John has a vision of 24 elders falling down before God, who sits on the throne of heaven,

worshiping and adoring Him as they cast their crowns at His feet. Read this Scripture. Imagine wearing an elegant crown you have been given, only by His grace and through faith, and now giving it back to the All-Worthy One. The gift of our crown pales in comparison to the gift of Jesus' life for ours. As you are overcome with a heart of profound gratitude for who Christ is and what He has done for you, pen your thoughts to Him.

Let's Pray

Faithful Father, You said that the only way we can come to know You is through Your Son, Jesus, because He is the Way, the Truth, and the Life. Like a scalpel to our dysfunctional heart, truth cuts away at the lies we've believed about ourselves. May Your voice, as a whisper or as a thunderous storm, drown out any deceitful voice we hear. Thank You for calling us a chosen, special treasure for Yourself. Teach us, Lord, what it means to love ourselves just as You love us, and fill us with Your perfect love. In Jesus' name, Amen.

Let's Sing:

Sing along with my sister on piano by scanning the QR code or visit my website under "Hymns in My Book."

authordeborahrodriguez.com

IDENTITY PURSUED

God had orchestrated life to reveal truth out of balance through my "false" perceptions. With the challenge from God's Word about the blessing Jabez asked for, my mind was jolted. I suddenly remembered a book about Jabez's prayer that had been sitting on my nightstand for about three months!

It was a setup by God. The busyness of home educating, church ministries, motherhood, and life in general kept me from reading it... until now. Eager and excited, I knew that I was to dive into this new assignment given by my Master Teacher.

Learning about the life and the prayer of Jabez was life-changing. I could identify with him. Jabez was a respected man but didn't really see himself that way. In I Chronicles 4:10 he petitioned God from the depths of his heart: *"Oh, that You would bless me indeed, and enlarge my territory, that Your hand would be with me, and that You would keep me from evil, that I may not cause pain!"* In verse 9 it says he was *"more honorable than his brothers, and his mother called his name Jabez,"* (meaning he causes pain), *"saying, 'Because I bore him in pain.'"*[8] At the end of verse 4:10, it says, *"So God granted him what he requested."*

---

[8] Bruce Wilkinson, *The Prayer of Jabez: Breaking Through to the Blessed Life* (Sisters, OR: Multnomah Publishers, 2000), 19.

In Biblical times, a person's name held a rich meaning. In Jewish culture, people believed that your name identified you. Can you imagine what kind of thoughts Jabez had growing up, knowing what his name meant? "I wonder why I cause problems everywhere I go?" Or, "How do other people perceive me?" Maybe people said, "Here comes trouble." Maybe people hid from him. Maybe he was a good kid and wondered about his purpose in life because of how he was perceived. His life would be impacted by his name.

I wonder if Jabez struggled to find significance in life. Earnestly pleading for blessing seems to go against the core meaning of his name. He didn't ask for a little, his petition was God-sized. Can you hear the desperate tone in his voice and feel the cry of his distressed heart, imploring the God of the universe to change the course of his future? "Oh, that You would bless me indeed..." In other words, "Don't just bless me. Bless me really big!" He didn't ask God to give someone else a huge blessing. He asked for himself. Selfish? I felt uncomfortable reading these words. Really uncomfortable. Observe how Jabez left it up to God to define what that ginormous blessing would be. He only wanted what God wanted—but he asked for himself. Stay with me if this makes you uncomfortable too.

Didn't Jesus say to ask? As obedient children, we should ask, knowing that just as a good earthly father delights in giving good gifts to his children, how much more so our heavenly Father (Matthew 7:11). I determined that when you look at your heritage (or your name) or your past and it seems to identify you because of experiences, circumstances, or lies you've believed about yourself, you may not believe you qualify for a blessing. Our God defies this false supposition.

Jabez refused to accept that his name would characterize his identity or future. Period.

In the next part of the prayer, Jabez asks for God to enlarge his territory. The word "territory" can also mean "borders" or "coast."[9] He did not covet more land. Instead, he wanted God to cause him to have a larger scope of influence. The meaning of his name, "he causes pain," may have kept him from impacting people's lives in a positive sense. Perhaps he wanted to break free of this stigma and influence more lives, not for his own glory, but for God's glory.

Does asking for more opportunity or influence for Christ sound intimidating? Frightening? Inspiring? Promising? Depending on who you are, the answer will be different. For me, it was, "I want to, but I have too many limitations." I saw my territory as small, with limits that I couldn't do anything about. In a way, it seemed humble to think this way. However, I was beginning to see that the more eternal effectiveness and influence I have, the more God gets the glory. We are blessed to be a blessing. I saw how my smallness gives God the opportunity to pour His all-sufficient grace and power on me so that He is glorified in His bigness. This brought me to an "Aha!" moment! Yes, my abilities, experiences, training, personality, past, heritage, mind, spirit, emotions, body, will—everything about me need not be downplayed as if it is humble to do so. These traits are God-given blessings and when used by Him, bring more honor, glory, and praise to Him. So, why not ask for more of this blessing?! This incited a sense of thrill and adventure inside me.

Jabez requested, "...that Your hand would be with me." Jabez knew, it seemed, that he would need God's mighty

---

[9] Ibid., 29.

hand to be with him if God was going to increase the impact he would be making in the lives of others for God's glory. I presume that this was a total paradigm shift for him, from small thinking to God-sized thinking; feelings of small value to big value. Weakness to strength. Inward to outward. Limited to limitless. His dependence on God caused him to wholeheartedly fling himself onto the power and grace of the same God that says, *"My grace is sufficient for you, for My strength is made perfect in weakness"* (2 Corinthians 12:9). Jabez thought, perhaps, as Paul did: *"Therefore, most gladly I will rather boast in my infirmities, that the power of Christ may rest upon me. Therefore, I take pleasure in infirmities, in reproaches, in needs, in persecutions, in distresses, for Christ's sake. For when I am weak, then I am strong"* (2 Corinthians 12:10). Do you ever feel like that? Imagine going from more blessing, more territory (influence), to more of God's presence (power). God is looking for opportunities to do this in us. *"For the eyes of the LORD run to and fro throughout the whole earth, to show Himself strong on behalf of those whose heart is loyal to Him"* (2 Chronicles 16:9a). Wholehearted, complete reliance on God equals His power and grace in my life.

Next, Jabez entreats *"...and that You would keep me from evil...."* Receiving more blessing, influence, and power can be a perfect situation for Satan to take advantage of us. We see from God's Word, history, and our present times how blessing, influence, and power can turn someone sour.[10] It has the potential to cause us to rely on self instead of the One who gave the blessing to us. The book of Daniel tells how the majestic Babylonian King Nebuchadnezzar became prideful

---

[10] Ibid., 63.

over the influence and blessings in his kingdom and lost them all as a result. Only by God's grace, and after Nebuchadnezzar repented, was he given back his kingdom. We may know of ministries or Christians that have been fruitful but because of moral failure, theft, pride, selfishness, or idolatry, they are no longer reputable (but still redeemable).

We can experience more attacks from Satan than ever before because we are messing with his territory, and he doesn't like it. These attacks can show up subtly in things such as distractions, sickness, discouragement, temptations, unfulfilled desires, or lust of the flesh, pride, and the lust of the eyes. I never really thought of praying to be kept from the battlefield. I always knew that we are soldiers in a battle (kingdom of darkness vs. the Kingdom of Light), to pray for strength to endure, and to pray for victory over sin and darkness. I never knew to pray that God would keep me away from temptation or to keep the devil and his legions away from us. If we are kept from temptation, it will help to prevent us from sinning.[11]

God's pursuing love was revealing my worth by teaching me that it's okay to ask for blessings just as Jabez did—for God's glory.   I committed to God that I would pray Jabez's prayer for 30 days. There was nothing magical about the number 30. I merely wanted to practice a discipline in this new spiritual paradigm, and to be accountable to the Lord for a committed amount of time initially.

God's pursuing love had positioned me to receive blessings beyond what my mind could have conceived, but though I didn't see it coming, the God of Breakthrough was about to unveil my heart even further. Through a trial

---

[11] Ibid., 67.

beyond my expectation and surpassing my capabilities, God orchestrated a life classroom to apply the principles I learned thus far. I was positioned to receive even more.

Key Take-Aways:

+ Jabez asked God for a God-sized blessing, despite how he or others identified him, for God's glory, and not for selfish reasons.

+ Let God define what that ginormous blessing is in your life.

+ An extensive territory (influence) equals a God-sized impact on others for Christ.

+ Our smallness gives God the opportunity to be our sufficient grace and power so that He is glorified in us in His bigness.

+ When God bestows more influence, He knows we will need His God-sized hand to be with us.

+ We can pray that God would keep us away from temptation or to keep the devil and his legions away from us.

Let's Reflect:

1. Read I Chronicles 4:9-10. Like Jabez, it's okay to ask God for a ginormous blessing for God's glory, to honor the true and living God. Contemplate that. Is there anything preventing you from taking hold of that truth? Write your thoughts.

2. What obstacles might keep you from trusting in a God-sized hand and His presence to be with you as you receive God's blessing? Confess your weaknesses or lack of faith so that God's strength and power

will operate within you. Read and meditate on 2 Corinthians 12:9-10. What is He saying to you?

3. We will always be tempted—even Jesus was! But you can ask God to keep you from temptation and the influence of Satan's schemes. Then, cooperate with His plan. Read 1 Corinthians 10:13. Jesus will make an escape from temptation. Write out your request.

Let's Pray:

Our pursuing God of love and redemption, cause us to hunger and thirst after You. Expose the condition in our hearts that won't allow us to receive Your matchless, bountiful blessings and rewards. Allow nothing to impede our heart to cry like Jabez, *"Oh, that You would bless me indeed, and enlarge my territory, that Your hand would be with me, and that You would keep me from evil, that I may not cause pain!"* God, grant us what we request for Your honor and glory. In Jesus' name, Amen.

Let's Sing:

Sing along with my sister on piano by scanning the QR code or visit my website under "Hymns in My Book."

authordeborahrodriguez.com

POSITIONED TO RECEIVE

*W*hile meditating on Jabez requesting that God abundantly bless him, I wondered—did he ask with a self-centered, ungrateful motive? No, it was pure. I determined that if Jabez could ask, I could ask too. My sense of worth was growing, but little did I know, God was positioning me to receive a ginormous blessing of my own.

"Deborah, I don't know what's wrong with your dad, but you need to come." I heard the trembling urgency in my dad's neighbor's voice over the phone. That sunny afternoon was like most spring afternoons in Wisconsin, but this particular one changed my life forever. With my heart racing, I bounded to the car to navigate to Dad's house while I prayed. When I burst into his living room, he began to speak in gibberish. With eyebrows furrowed, his arms flailing in the air, and eyes widened with anxiety he attempted to communicate his experience. It was apparent that he suffered a stroke. I called 911. After the paramedics' assessment, they strapped him securely onto the gurney and transported him and me to the hospital he frequented, where the diagnosis was confirmed. It was surreal. Just that morning, I committed to praying the Jabez prayer for 30 days. Feeling numb with unbelief that this was happening, I prayed for my dad but announced to God that this was *not* my idea of Him blessing me—or "expanding my borders." Through the crisis, I remembered that He defines what blessing is — not me. Filled with hope, I began to use my spiritual eyes to look for the blessing and envision how He would expand my borders and bless me indeed.

Life was altered significantly. My husband immediately took on the responsibilities of a home without me as I had the blessing of rooming with my dad at the hospital over the next few weeks. My six children, ages 11-25 years, acquired some new assignments and skills that caused them to grow and mature as they attended to each other's needs. Fortunately, it was the end of the school year, and thankfully, my willing husband and industrious children held the fort down, though it was difficult for them. I will be forever grateful for this gift they gave to me as I utilized my abilities as a registered nurse for a most treasured "patient."

After 27 days of hospitalization, including rehab, we journeyed back to his home, where he was mandated to have 24/7 supervision. My family allowed me the blessing and honor of tending to this need. Since I was a teenager, I always dreamed of caring for my parents in their old age. Though bittersweet, I was greatly appreciative to be in a position of giving back to my dad in some small way. Strength flowed out of the joy I experienced. I packed my belongings, expressed very difficult goodbyes to my family, and equipped myself with two life-giving books: my Bible and a book by David Wilkerson entitled *Knowing God by Name: Names of God That Bring Hope and Healing.*

I was on the lookout for God to define that blessing and reward, as I learned from Jabez. Getting information from my dad about his life while I lived with him was painstakingly difficult. He is not only a very private man, but it took great effort for him to understand me and express himself. It was a situation that positioned me to depend on God in a way that I had never known before. I entered the world of caring for a senior citizen, spending most of my time trying to communicate in a way that he could understand and the rest of the time learning from scratch what it meant to be a durable power of attorney for finances and healthcare. I felt ill-equipped to deal with the reality before me, yet what I *did* have going for me was a deep loving relationship with my dad, faith in a mighty God to teach me what good was going to come out of it all, and praying family and friends.

As time permitted, I read the two books I packed. The verse, *"Our help is in the **name** of the LORD, who made heaven and earth"* (Psalm 124:8, emphasis added) grew to have new meaning in my life. A strong foundation was laid for me as I studied the truth of God's Word concerning who He is through His names and attributes. Where His name was once concealed or overlooked in the past, it now became enthroned and exalted in my heart.

It wasn't just a study in the knowledge of His names. Intimacy and relationship were kindled in experiencing Him as Jehovah Jireh, The LORD Will Provide; Jehovah Shalom, The LORD is Peace; El Shaddai, The All-Sufficient One; Elohei Mikkarov, the God Who is Near; and Jehovah Gibbor Milchamah, The LORD Mighty in Battle. 'El' indicates the great power of God, and 'Jehovah' suggests "to become known" or implies a God who reveals Himself unceasingly.[12]

"Deborah, I want you to have my car. I can't drive it anymore." My dad had purchased a brand new Chevy Cruze just a couple of months before his stroke. Bewildered, I quickly replied, "No, Dad, I can't take your car. That's your car. You're going to get better and drive it again someday."

---

[12] Gospel Tract Society, *I Am That I Am: YHWH* (Independence, MO: Gospel Tract Society, n.d.).

Dad brought up accepting his car several times during the summer that I stayed with him. Every time, I had the same reply, "No, Dad, I can't take your car. That's your car. You're going to get better and drive it again someday."

One morning, my dad firmly announced, "We are going to the motor vehicle department." Out of respect, I consented. I knew he meant business, and I discerned there would be no reasoning with him. Seated in the motor vehicle department, I couldn't wrap my mind around getting a brand-new car from my dad. A war was going on inside. I reasoned, "I'll get the title and license plate to honor Dad, but it's still his car." Soon I walked out with the title and license plate in hand. Casually tossing them in the trunk of his car, I confidently mused under my breath, "I pleased him," but I had not accepted the gift in my heart. To me, it was still his car, not mine.

Our bond grew stronger that summer. I was beyond blessed to care for my dad, yet I had spent many days trying to separate my real dad from my "stroke dad." He was working through his new way of communicating, and I was learning how to understand him. He was still my special dad. We were both dealing with a "new normal," and it was tough. Really tough. We were both grieving our losses in our own way. I, through many tears, and him, through anger, yet I knew that this too would pass in time. In God's foresight, this was the soil that brought the miracle of knowing my royal identity in Christ to fruition.

After two months passed, my dad got clearance to be unsupervised for a few hours in the evenings. Happy day! I was free to go home for a window of time to visit my family and serve them. Once home, I sensed the weight of my absence and plunged in to alleviate as much burden as possible by cleaning, completing housework, catching up on conversations and personal experiences, and hugs. I shed many tears of joy from being able to see family and attend to their needs, but something wasn't right with me. I couldn't put a finger on it. I couldn't function as usual.

Grateful as he was to have me care for him, Dad knew I couldn't stay with him forever. So, with the help of my sister, who lived out of state, we inquired about different retirement communities and then moved him into one nearby. This was yet another emotionally difficult day of our lives. No one prepared my dad or I for this difficult day of saying goodbye to my childhood home, and to the home that he had resided in for 60 years.

Two days later, my husband got a call that his father was in hospice with kidney failure, so I went to meet him in Illinois. After 27 years of visiting my in-laws, my mind was unclear on how to get there. I had to ask a friend to drive me there, and I couldn't read the map. In a brief moment of alarm, I questioned, *Wow, what's wrong with me?* but quickly forgot about it as I focused on the next opportunity to serve. Arriving there, I was so happy to minister in any way and offered to my sister-in-law, "Let me know how I can help. I'm willing to be a gopher, make a meal, or help with anything."

After shedding tears and connecting with family, my 11-year-old daughter and I went to my sister-in-law's house later that evening to sleep. When I woke up the next morning, I could barely move. I cried, not for myself, but because I couldn't do what I had offered. I couldn't keep my word. Deeply disappointed, I had to express to my sister-in-law that I was honestly not able to function. In the days following, I had to take two naps each day.

I thought that it was just a physical problem until one night during the two weeks we were there, I got a new game out to play with my daughter, just to give her a diversion from our grieving. After reading the first two or three sentences of the instructions three times in a row, it alarmed me that I didn't understand a word I read–- but I brushed it aside. The focus was on my family as they came to visit my father-in-law as he slowly slipped away. It disturbed me that I could not fully support the family in the capacity that I wanted to. I barely had the energy to grieve the loss of my kind, gentle father-in-law when his life finally came to an end.

Upon arriving home, I realized I had no physical, emotional, or mental energy to serve my grieving husband and six precious children. I was still taking two naps a day and had to conserve energy to make meals and connect with my family that I had barely seen for two and a half months. Was this God's idea of expanding my borders? I was discouraged. Happy to be home, yet unable to function as a wife and mother, I prayed, "God, I don't know what's happening to me, but I know You have a purpose for this. Please reveal Your purpose."

The spiritual foundation that was laid while living with my dad was sure and strong. I knew that I could trust God's loving heart because He is Jehovah, the One who had unceasingly revealed Himself to me through challenges that extended me far beyond my own strength. Jehovah Jireh, The LORD will Provide, was not far away. He was near. My impossibilities became His opportunity to be faithful to who He was. I found a resting place in Him like the peace and calm that is in the eye of a storm.

Though I was unaware of God's perfect plan in the days ahead, He had positioned me to receive even more.The God-sized blessing was about to be revealed. My significance was set free.

Key Take-Aways:

+ God positions us, often with challenges and trials, to experience a facet of His character through His names that we never experienced before.

+ Unanswered questions in our lives give us the opportunity to cling to the One who has the answers.

+ As we grow in the knowledge of God's names and character, we can grow in faith that God will bring a powerful testimony out of our trials for His glory.

+ We can trust God's loving heart even when we don't see His hand.

+ Our impossibilities can become God's opportunity to be faithful to who He is if we surrender to His loving heart. Our resting place in Him is like the peace and calm that is in the eye of a storm.

Let's Reflect:

1. What trial, circumstance, ailment, or "cross" do you face in your life; something so big and beyond your measure physically, mentally, emotionally, or spiritually? Will you consider that He may be positioning you to experience Him as never before through His name? Record these overwhelming odds in your journal and then, by faith, ask God to reveal His purposes. Trust His loving heart even when you

don't see His hand at work. Write an honest prayer to sincerely dedicate yourself to trust Him.

2. Could God be preparing you through your trials today to be a stronger soldier tomorrow? Could your test be God positioning you to allow Him to make you into a testimony of His grace? What is He saying to you?

3. What is God orchestrating in your life, even in your questions, to allow God's glory to shine through you? Ask Him. Then pen them.

Let's Pray:

Position us, Lord, to say, *"Unite my heart to fear Your name,"* (Psalm 86:11b). Instead of pushing away our trials in life, posture our hearts to receive the faith to believe that You are in the storm, orchestrating our lives to know You more intimately. We trust that You are always good. In Jesus' name, Amen.

Let's Sing:

Sing along with my sister on piano by scanning the QR code or visit my website under "Hymns in My Book."

authordeborahrodriguez.com

IDENTITY RECOVERED

$\mathcal{G}$od was planning another setup. Being positioned in my weakness was key for me to receive more blessing. After arriving home from the funeral in Illinois, I mustered the energy to visit my dad. The toll of exhaustion and grieving for my father-in-law weighed heavily. As we walked outside his apartment complex on a beautiful September day, he asked, "What car did you drive today?" Pointing across the street, I apologetically affirmed, "That one." He detected my old, rusty, 15-passenger van and bellowed in frustration, "Don't bring that back here!" Uh-oh, he noticed that I hadn't driven his car! Although I owned the title and new license plate, they were still in the trunk of his car in his garage (Have you noticed that I was still calling it his car?). I knew then that I would have to drive his car the next time I visited him.

We had always owned a family-sized van with the bare minimum of accessories, driving it until it almost fell apart, and then would buy another used van. So, I knew that in my mental and physical exhaustion, it would be more than a challenge to read and understand the instruction book on how to drive this $30,000 car with all the "bells and whistles." Fortunately, a close friend of the family agreed to instruct me.

My youngest daughter and I met him at my dad's house. I was instructed to take the car out of the garage and park it in the driveway so that he could coach me. My heart screamed as I drew near the garage door, "I don't want to do this!" Reluctantly, I approached the driver's door, unlocked it, and slid into the luxurious seat. It felt very foreign and uncomfortable. Almost surreal. I didn't like sitting in his extravagant gift. I felt like I didn't belong there. Unnatural. I wanted to flee, but the overcoming thought was, *I must do this to see Dad again, to make him happy.*

What transpired next was never experienced in the measure it was that day. It was unexpected. It felt "otherworldly" to turn the key in the ignition. In that moment, a mighty dam of God's love suddenly broke open—immeasurable, incalculable, infinite love. I wept. Uncontrollably. I had never wept as such before. The awesomeness of God's endless love could not be contained.

Overwhelmingly humbled and awe-struck, I didn't know what to do. Weak from mental, emotional, and physical exhaustion and now overwhelmingly awestruck and overcome with God's presence, I needed to be alone. Alone with Him. The Lover of My Soul. I staggered as if intoxicated past my friend, then unsteadily winding past my daughter painting a picture at the kitchen table, I fell onto the bed. I wept until I could weep no more.

The message was clear. God was speaking to my heart. It was distinct, unmistakable, and authentic. "Just as your dad gave you this costly gift out of his pain and suffering, I too, have given My love to you out of My pain and suffering. And you are worth it." The price of God's love through the gift of His Son, who gave His life for me so that I could have life eternal with Him and life abundant on this earth, was incomprehensible. He exposed how my feelings of insignificance had prevented me from stepping foot in that garage to drive that car. The picture in my mind was tangible. There were levels of His vast love that I had not experienced until then. "Deborah, just as you did nothing to earn this car, you merely need to receive this vast love. You are worth it. Yes, everybody you have served over the years was worth it, and I understand that you love Me, and out of that love you serve Me. But I want you to really *know* that I value *you*. *You* are significant. *You* are cherished. *You* are treasured and prized as My precious child. *You* are a child of the King of Kings. I delight in *you,* not just those you serve!"

God peeled away the layers of my heart that had kept me from His ever-deepening love. I grew up in a loving, Christian home where God and His Word were exalted. I sang the song "Jesus Loves Me, This I Know" from the time I was a toddler. Before we fell asleep each night, my mother read that precious Book, the Holy Bible, to my sister and me before we could read. I have read God's Word since I learned how to read. I went to church every Sunday morning, Sunday night, and Wednesday night. I asked Jesus into my heart at the age of five. I had taught about His love since I was 12 years of age. I served Him in some capacity most of my life, yet this depth of His love and the feeling of significance and worth was not experienced until now.

Wiping my tears and composing myself as well as I could, I went back outside and explained to my friend what had taken place before his eyes. I felt embarrassed. He merely came to help me learn how to drive a car and unexpectedly witnessed an emotional and spiritual breakthrough! He sensitively listened as I explained to him why tears flooded my eyes the moment I turned the key in the ignition. After a few words of acknowledgment, we then turned our attention to learning how to navigate all the basic buttons I needed to know to drive the car. In my altered mental and physical state, it took nearly an hour and a half to finally comprehend the instructions. After we went for a test drive, I finally felt equipped to visit my dad that week.

That week's visit included taking him to a doctor's appointment. On the way there, he brought up the subject of the car. In our conversation I reminded him that it was still his car and—yes, you can guess what I said—that someday he would drive it again. With crinkled eyebrows and voice raised in anger, he emphatically proclaimed, "If I want a car, I'll buy a car!"

I was stunned and speechless. It was as if God was proclaiming to me, "It's sealed! The car is no longer your dad's car, it's *yours!* There's no turning back. No adjustments, excuses, or otherwise. I have obliterated all the perceptions and beliefs in your mind of your insignificance. You are an heir to My throne, a child of the Most High God. Deborah, I love to lavish My love not only on others but also on you. My inheritance is yours, just as this car is your inheritance from your dad. Receive it." At that moment, something changed inside of me. I experienced the Deliverer rescuing me from the lies I believed about myself, and He gave me hope. God's pursuing love had positioned me to receive. The car was no longer "Dad's car," it was *mine!* More importantly, the car was a visible reminder to me of who God calls me and Whose I am.

My identity in Christ was recovered, and *He* was my reward! I was experiencing God as Abba Father and Lover of My Soul. I was experiencing His pursuing love for me as a cherished child of the Most High God—royalty! His presence and intimacy were being experienced at a level I had never experienced before. I finally embraced my valuable significance in His eyes.

Do you have difficulty accepting God's love for you? Ponder carefully Ephesians 3:14-21:

> *"For this reason I bow my knees to the Father of our Lord Jesus Christ, from whom the whole family in heaven and earth is named, that He would grant you, according to the riches of His glory, to be strengthened with might through His Spirit in the inner man, that Christ may dwell in your hearts through faith; that you, being rooted and grounded in love, may be able to comprehend with all the saints what is the width and length and depth and height—to know the love of Christ which passes knowledge; that you may be filled with all the fullness of God. Now to Him who is able to do exceedingly abundantly above all that we ask or think, according to the power that works in us, to Him be glory in the church by Christ Jesus to all generations, forever and ever. Amen."*

In our walk with God, many times, it's through trial and suffering that He shares more of His intimacy with us. He reveals secrets to us and mysteries we would have never understood unless we were positioned to receive this gift of experiencing Him. We can choose to run into the arms of Jesus during these times or we can flee. As in the above verses, we come to Him in a bowing posture of our heart—humbled. He is the God who created the universe, giving us the very breath in our lungs. According to the riches of His glory, He desires to strengthen us with His might through His Spirit in our inner man. We like to claim our own strength and determination, yet He is the One who gave it to us.

Christ in all of His resurrection power lives in us and desires to dwell in our hearts through faith. When we are rooted and grounded in Christ's love, it continuously grows wider, longer, deeper, and higher. His endless love surpasses knowledge, so that we may be filled with all the fullness of God as we grow in His deep, deep love. It is this God—Jesus Christ-who is able to do above and beyond what we ask or think, according to His power that we allow to work in us! To Him be praise!

Will you permit Him to allow your trials to turn into triumph? Your test into a testimony? Weakness into strength? Insignificance into significance? You may feel insignificant, but the truth is, you are highly treasured. The God of the universe pursues you, through a relationship with Jesus Christ!

What do you need God to break through in your life for you to allow Him to be your Reward? We can trust with the Psalmist, *"You will show me the path of life; in Your presence is fullness of joy; at Your right hand are pleasures forevermore"* (Psalm 16:11). When His presence becomes everything to us (through His name), our trials turn to gold and meaning in life springs out of empty confusion. He will show us the path of life. The presence of our Almighty God brings us joy and pleasures forevermore. What can you trust Him for in your situation? Come into His presence knowing His pursuing love. Let Him give you words of Truth to recover your identity.

With my identity in Christ firmly rooted and sealed now, there were still other parts that needed healing. God's pursuing love ushered in deeper healing.

Key Take-Aways:

✦ God positions us in our weakness to receive more of Him.

✦ God can peel away the layers of our hearts that block us from His ever-deepening love.

✦ God will imprint in our heart and mind the truth in God's Word that we are who He says we are—an heir to His throne, a Child of the Most High God.

✦ God yearns to bless His children.

✦ Knowing our identity in Christ changes everything when we see ourselves the way He sees us.

✦ *God*, in all of His attributes through His names, *is our Reward!*

Let's Reflect:

1. Read and meditate on Ephesians 3:14-21. Personalize this passage,create it as a prayer in your journal, and then pray it for yourself. For example: "I bow my knees to You, Father, and thank You that You would grant the riches of Your glory to strengthen me with might through Your Spirit in my inner man. I ask that Christ will make His dwelling place in my heart through faith, and being rooted and grounded in Your love, I may be able to comprehend how wide, long, deep, and high Your love is. I want to know the love of Christ which surpasses knowledge so I may be filled with all the fullness of God. You are able to do exceedingly abundantly above all that I ask or think, according to the power that works in me. I give You glory. In Jesus' name, Amen."

2. Read and meditate on Psalm 16:11. Ask God to plant a seed in your heart to begin to trust Him through all of His names. Practice the presence of God throughout

your day. Allow trials to be a springboard of entering into His presence where there is fullness of joy. Compose your prayer.

3. Ask the God of Breakthrough, Jehovah Baal Perez, to break through any hindrance of receiving His vast love for you. Ask Him to help you see yourself the way He sees you. Journal your thoughts and prayers.

Let's Pray:

God, Your pursuing love never diminishes. While we were yet sinners, You sent Your Son, Jesus, to die for us. When we didn't even know we needed more of You, You positioned us to receive even more of You. The more of You we experience, the more of You we want to experience. Your measureless, pursuing love cannot be contained, nor can it be consumed. Thank You for blessing us with the trials in our lives to cause us to experience You in aspects we never have before. The treasure of experiencing You far outweighs the trial we undergo. In Jesus' name, Amen.

Let's Sing:

Sing along with my sister on piano by scanning the QR code or visit my website under "Hymns in My Book."

authordeborahrodriguez.com

PROFOUND HEALING

*W*ith my identity recovered through the flood of God's love, I still needed deeper healing, and not just in my spirit. After some research, it came to my attention that I might be dealing with adrenal exhaustion or burnout. Lying on my bed exhausted after doing little one day, the Scripture came to my mind, *"Is anyone among you sick? Let him call for the elders of the church, and let them pray over him, anointing him with oil in the name of the Lord. And the prayer of faith will save the sick, and the Lord will raise him up. And if he has committed sins, he will be forgiven"* (James 5:14-15). Weak and feeble, I went to the Wednesday night prayer meeting and shared a bit about my condition. I requested to be anointed with oil for healing. The small faithful group, which I identify as some of my dearest friends, gathered around. Each one prayed for healing while I was anointed with oil by the pastor, my husband. Nothing spectacular happened, but I trusted in Jehovah-Rapha, God my Healer.

The next day, I awoke and sailed through my day energetically. Feeling rested, I prepared breakfast, home-educated, cleaned and organized the house, and threw a lunch together. I felt emotionally, mentally, and physically capable of managing my responsibilities. By evening, a light bulb turned on! It dawned on me that I was not only healed but functioning in a capacity greater, by far, than I did before being my dad's caregiver. *"Now to Him who is able to do exceedingly abundantly above all that we ask or think, according to the power that works in us, to Him be glory in the church by Christ Jesus to all generations, forever and ever. Amen"* (Ephesians 3:20-21). I had asked for healing so I could serve my family, but He had given me more than I asked for. I possessed mental, emotional, physical, and spiritual energy I didn't know existed. Only someone who has been healed by the mighty hand of God knows the overwhelming feeling and awe of the moment they experience healing that only God could have performed.

God, in His faithfulness, healed my mind exceedingly abundantly. This was evident the day I took my youngest daughter to see her orthopedic doctor for a checkup. After looking at an X-ray of her right femur and hip, he said she would need yet another surgery. My heart hit the floor. She was eleven years old and already had surgery eight times for bone issues. I began asking the doctor questions that surprised even me. I didn't know where they were coming from! He looked at the X-ray again and audibly rehearsed his mathematical calculations. With a serious, almost bewildered look, he swiveled around in his chair, announcing, "She doesn't need surgery after all." Glory, Hallelujah! No explanation needed! I knew that God had put His wisdom in me to ask those questions to turn history around for our daughter! With tears of joy and reverent awe, I praised God all the way home.

God also purified and cleansed my will. Before God's healing, I was so fatigued that I barely had the will to do the next thing. That state of exhaustion was the soil in which I was positioned to receive a deeper understanding, sensitivity, and more profound distinction between doing what Deborah wanted and doing what God wanted. Any will of my own, even to do good, was as filthy rags if I didn't give glory and credit to God. I sensed that God took the strength of my own will and replaced it with the bountiful goodness and powerful enablement of His will. I had believed a truth out of balance that *I* needed to will to do what is right and true. Philippians 2:12-13 explains the whole truth:

⚜   *"Work out your **own** salvation with fear and trembling; for it is **God** who works in you both to will and to do for His good pleasure."* (emphasis added)

The New Living Translation says it this way:

⚜   "Work hard to show the results of your salvation, obeying God with deep reverence and fear. For God is working in you, giving you the desire and the power to do what pleases Him."

In verse 12, Paul gives admonition to work diligently at what salvation needs to practically look like in our own lives, with reverence and fear of God. Then in verse 13, he says that *God* is working in us to give us the desire and the power to do what pleases God. To focus on one more than the other could lead us to rely on our own strength, or to place the whole responsibility on the moving of the Holy Spirit to carry out the will of God in our life. This is truth out of balance. There must be a cooperation of our diligence to work out our own salvation, and His working in us to will and to do His good pleasure.

God gave me a good dose of I John 4:10: *"In this is love, not that we loved God, but that He loved us and sent His Son to be the propitiation for our sins."* It was His love that pursued me and delivered me from sin—I didn't have anything to do with it. My lopsided focus had been too far on the end of diligently working out my salvation with fear and trembling, instead of including how much He delighted in giving me the desire and power to do what pleases Him.

Scriptures began to jump out at me about God taking pleasure in enabling us to do His will and gain His attributes. For example, these two verses:

* *"**Guard** your heart above all else, for it determines the course of your life"* (Proverbs 4:23, NLT, emphasis added).

* *"and **the peace of God,** which surpasses all understanding, **will guard** your hearts and minds through Christ Jesus"* (Phillipians 4:7, emphasis added).

Notice that in Proverbs *we* are the ones to guard our hearts. In Philippians, it is (the peace of) *God* who will guard our hearts and minds through Christ Jesus.

Here is another example:

* *"**let us draw near** with a true heart in full assurance of faith, having our hearts sprinkled from an evil conscience and our bodies washed with pure water"* (Hebrews 10:22, emphasis added).

* *"But now in Christ Jesus **you** who once were far off **have been brought near by the blood of Christ"** (Ephesians 2:13, emphasis added).

In Hebrews, it is we who draw near. In Ephesians, it is the blood of Christ which has brought us near. God pursues us and we have a responsibility to choose to respond.

One more:

✿ *"For this very reason,* **make every effort** *to add to your faith, goodness; and to goodness, knowledge; and to knowledge, self-control; and to self-control, perseverance; and to perseverance, godliness; and to godliness, mutual affection; and to mutual affection, love." "...***make every effort** *to confirm your calling and election"* (2 Peter 1:5-7, 10 NIV, emphasis added).

✿ *"***His divine power** *has given us everything we need for a godly life through our knowledge of Him who called us by His own glory and goodness"* (2 Peter 1:3 NIV, emphasis added).

In verses 5-7 and 10, we make the effort. In verse 3, it is God's divine power. I didn't give up one truth for the other, I only balanced them. Spiritual cleansing took place in that time of healing that I never asked for nor expected. His power, His might, His enabling in my life grew. His yoke was easier, His burden lighter. My heart was light, free, forgiven, cleansed, new, like a clean slate ready for God to write His new life story on. There was a sweet rest.

He gave me exceedingly, abundantly, more than I asked or thought. In response to His lavish love and blessing, praise and worship flowed freely toward Him. Emotionally and spiritually, the joy of the Lord was my strength, and in His presence was a fullness of joy experienced as never before. The oneness in intimacy with God, whom I had served most of my life, was beyond description. I experienced Him as Jehovah Rapha, my Healer. I felt like a superhero in Christ!

Often, God allows our weaknesses or frailties to awaken us to the fact that He is our strength. He is Healer. Paul, in the book of II Corinthians 12:9 declares, *"And He said to me, 'My grace is sufficient for you, for My strength is made perfect in weakness.' Therefore most gladly I will rather boast in my infirmities, that the power of Christ may rest upon me."* We can boast with Paul and say we take pleasure in these infirmities, reproaches, and needs, persecutions, and distresses for Christ's sake. For when we are weak (physically, mentally, emotionally, or spiritually), then we are strong (in Christ). The entire healing caused my heart to be enlarged to receive even more blessings from Him. My spiritual eyes were transformed to look for Him and His blessings more steadfastly.

The one who previously couldn't receive, now through God's pursuing love, was led into a season of receiving. Not only materially, but more importantly, mentally, spiritually, and emotionally.

Key Take-Aways:

+ God desires a profound healing in our life. Don't settle for partial restoration. God is still working!

+ God seeks to impart His great delight in His children by doing "exceeding abundantly" more than we ask or think.

+ Truth out of balance is not valid truth.

+ We must work diligently at what our salvation needs to look like in the fear of the Lord while acknowledging that God is working in us to give us the desire and power to do what pleases Him.

+ God longs to enlarge our hearts to receive more blessings from Him.

+ God's lavish blessings result in praise and worship to Him more freely (and so much more).

Let's Reflect:

1. Are you focused more on what *you* "will" to do for God, or on *His* divine power to live a godly life? Ask the Lord to bring your focus into balance. Search the Word of God to align your heart to His definition of truth. Here are some starters: 1) Proverbs 4:23 and Philippians 4:7; 2) Hebrews 10:22 and Ephesians 2:13; 3) 2 Peter 1:5-7, 10 and 2 Peter 1:3. Record your findings and design your prayer.

2. What in your life has God allowed as a weakness or limitation? Could He be allowing this weakness to turn your eyes on Him as the All-Sufficient One? Write down what you sense to surrender to God, and His grace will meet you right there.

3. We all need healing in our life, whether it is physical, mental, emotional, or spiritual. Physically, it could be an ailment, disease, or pain. Mentally, it could be lies or deception we've believed, ungodly thoughts, or bad memories. Emotionally, it could be feelings of abandonment, grief, rejection, or depression. Spiritually, it could be a heart of sinfulness, worldliness, or need of deliverance from bondage. Humbly ask God to heal you through the anointing of oil as Scripture says. Mark a day on the calendar to do this.

Let's Pray:

God, our Healer and Restorer above what we can ask or imagine, we thank You for Your desire to make us *completely* whole. Peel away the layers of our heart to reveal the lies we've believed, and allow Your truth to reign. Cause us to not only work out our own salvation but also yield to Your power and desire to do what pleases You. May we glory in our weakness so Your power will reign in us for Your glory and honor. In Jesus' name, Amen.

Let's Sing:

Sing along with my sister on piano by scanning the QR code or visit my website under "Hymns in My Book."

authordeborahrodriguez.com

SEASON OF RECEIVING

$\mathcal{A}$s I experienced Jehovah-Rapha—God my Healer, He led me into a season of accepting and welcoming His blessings more easily. The one who had served for years without feeling significant enough to receive was now learning how to accept God as One who delights in blessing and reward. It was a complete mind shift.

Going about my regular duties one day, the Lord brought to my attention the money I received as birthday gifts and giftings for the pastor's wife for the last 25 years. Every time I had received an envelope with only my name written on it, I put it aside. My motive was to honestly honor the gift giver who wanted me, specifically, to have it rather than the family. With my new mindset, the Lord revealed to me that when I received the monetary gift, it went directly into a hiding place because I could not fathom that I was worth having it. After counting the hidden treasure, it tallied $5,000!

Again, overcome by His delight in me, I wept. His recurring message to me confirmed who and Whose I am. He was taking me from a pauper mentality to a mindset of royalty— a child of the King of Kings! I knew I was not worthy, but He was clearly stamping an imprint on my mind of my precious value. Undoubtedly, He didn't want me just to count the gift money, but to spend some of it. So, taking $3 to K-mart, I purchased my favorite store-bought cookies—Pepperidge Farm Double

Chocolate Milano cookies! I ate almost the whole bag myself, sharing none of them! It felt foreign.

My speech even changed, and not by my own doing! After my dad moved out of his house, friends and loved ones rummaged through his house to take what they saw of value. A friend called me one day and remarked, "Deborah, we returned the furnace filters to K-Mart from your dad's house. They gave us an $83 gift card as a refund. We would like to give it to you. My husband would like to drop it off." Normally I would have refused the gift and been elated that I could bless them, so I started to respond, "Oh, no, that's okay, I'm so blessed that you came to take what you wanted from my dad's house. It means less work for me to dispose of it..." But this time, God changed my answer in mid-sentence. I laughed in my spirit. My healed mind was already declaring to my mouth what to speak! I continued, "*But,* though it would give me joy to have you keep the gift card as a thank you, I'm guessing it would bring you just as much joy to bless me with it." She agreed! I was learning to allow others to have the joy of giving to me, without feeling insignificant.

Getting rid of the belongings left behind in my dad's house provoked another emotional roller coaster ride because some of my treasured childhood possessions were among them. It was not possible to keep them since there was no room in our house. Yet, one of the biggest, most meaningful gifts I received was the help at the end of this sentimental journey. I realized at this point in the process that I needed help, so I felt the freedom now to ask my prayer group and my sister Ruth to finish the sizable task. My sister and her children, Jonathan and Rosie, came from Connecticut and spent a week coordinating the project. They completely emptied the house to get it ready to sell. My business-minded sister then took the responsibility of selling the house. That heavy burden was lifted through her expertise. I am forever grateful.

After the close of that chapter in my life, within a few weeks, I pursued updating my RN license. I hadn't been employed for 25 years as a registered nurse, putting nursing on hold for the greater honor and blessing of home-educating our six children. Now, the same mind that could not comprehend the instructions in a child's game several weeks earlier was taking a refresher course, including three weeks of theory and skills in the classroom and five weeks of clinicals at a rehab unit. Although nervous, I went forward knowing I had experienced healing in body and mind. Over and over, I sang praise to God for His infinite mercy as I traveled to and from training in the "sanctuary" (my car) that I call "a hug from God."

My car has been like a mouthpiece of God in the lessons of life regarding this new facet of relating to Him. One day, after taking my car to get an oil change at the dealership, I decided to swing by and visit the salesman who sold the car to my dad. Heartbrokenly, I mentioned that my dad suffered a stroke and that I was now the owner of the car. Expressing his considerate thoughtfulness, he then let me in on a very humbling piece of information. "Your dad bought his last two cars here knowing that you would eventually be the owner." My eyes welled up with tears. I was reminded once again of God's bountiful love. Just as I was unaware of my earthly father's loving thoughts toward me, so too my Heavenly Father's thoughts toward me are beyond measure. *"How precious also are Your thoughts to me, O God! How great is the sum of them! If I should count them, they would be more in number than the sand..."* (Psalm 139:17-18).

Oh, the wondrous reminder of His immeasurable loving thoughts toward us when we are not even mindful of Him! *"When I consider Your heavens, the work of Your fingers, the moon and the stars, which You have ordained, what is man that You are mindful of him, and the son of man that You visit him? For You have made him a little lower than the angels, and You have crowned him with glory and honor"* (Psalm 8:3-5). I am always on His mind. Ceaselessly. Continuously. Endlessly.

This truth hit home hard after reading a selection by Robert Munger. In his short story, coined "My Heart - Christ's Home," Munger appeals to the Christian to completely consecrate himself to the Lord and enthrone Christ to be at home in every area of his heart. Together, Jesus and the owner of the house (which depicts our heart), visit the library, dining room, workshop, playroom, and even a cupboard where the man has a hidden area he didn't at first want Him to see.

What took place in the drawing-room affected me the most. This room was described as "intimate and comfortable." It was a place of sweet fellowship, and Jesus asked the owner to come here to begin every day with Him. The owner couldn't think of a better idea than to intimately connect with Christ in this way. Every morning, Jesus would declare the beautiful promises and truths of His Word, and the owner's heart was drawn to Jesus' love and grace. As life does, the responsibilities and pressures of living caused the owner to miss the special time in the drawing-room, at first on occasion, then more regularly. Until one day...[13]

---

[13] Paraphrase of *My Heart — Christ's Home* by Robert Boyd Munger, copyright © 1986 by InterVarsity Christian Fellowship of the United States of America. Used by permission of InterVarsity Press, https://www.ivpress.com.

The owner of the house expressed, "I remember one morning when I was rushing downstairs, eager to be on my way, that I passed the drawing room and noticed that the door was ajar. Looking in, I saw a fire in the fireplace and the Master sitting there next to it. Suddenly, in dismay I thought to myself, *He is my guest. I invited him into my heart! He has come, and yet I am neglecting Him.*

With downcast glance, I said, "Blessed Master, forgive me. Have You been here all these mornings?"

"Yes," He said. "I told you I would be here every morning to meet with you. Remember, I love you. I have redeemed you at great cost. I desire your fellowship. Even if you cannot keep the quiet time for your own sake, do it for Mine."[14]

"The truth that Christ desires my companionship, that He wants me to be with Him and waits for me, has done more to transform my quiet time with God than any other single factor. Don't let Christ wait alone in the drawing-room of your heart, but every day find time when, with your Bible and in prayer, you may have fellowship with Him."[15]

The God of the universe is seeking us for companionship, fellowship, communion, intimacy, relationship, union, and closeness! He desires us! Delights over us! Takes pleasure in us! Savors a relationship with us! Revels in enjoying our companionship! How heart-wrenching it must be for our Creator to see us only *doing* what pleases Him when He longs for us to just *be* in His presence for Him to enjoy *our* presence! It's one thing to experience the God who sits on the throne as King of our life. It's a whole new level of understanding when you experience Him as the God who extends His

---

[14] Robert Boyd Munger, *My Heart — Christ's Home*, copyright © 1986 by InterVarsity Christian Fellowship of the United States of America. Used by permission of InterVarsity Press, https://www.ivpress.com.

[15] Ibid.

scepter to you, saying, "I see you, I want you, you are worth more than a million gold mines, you are the apple of My eye, your name is written on the palm of My hands, I love you with an everlasting love." What a mind-shift this was for me! Again, without discounting the fact that it is vital to obey Him and serve Him, I never really pondered His delight in being in *my* presence, enjoying *my* company and longing for *me* even more than I do for Him. This truth received and planted deep in my heart compelled me to respond by embracing Him and seeking Him as one who longs to commune with their lover.

The season of receiving taught me to be more accepting, welcoming, and even requesting God's blessings and rewards. Although material blessings were accepted, they paled in light of embracing the blessed thought that He enjoys and delights in my presence, seeks intimacy with me, and desires relationship. As my thinking was transformed, it paved the way for a metamorphosis in how I saw myself.

Key Take-Aways:

✦ God takes great pleasure in revealing who He is and who we are in Christ.

✦ God's manifold loving, precious thoughts towards us are impossible to count. They are as numerous as the grains of sand in the sea (Psalm 139:17-18).

✦ Our value is not dependent on our feelings or what a man or demon may say about us. At the foot of the cross, our value is fixed—forever.

✦ Although material blessings are accepted, they pale in light of embracing the blessed thought that God enjoys and delights in our presence, seeks us for intimacy, and desires relationship.

Let's Reflect:

1. Learning to receive. Let that soak in for a moment. Have you had a time in your life when you wanted to run from the gift giver? The Lord has exposed times in my past that I graciously said, "Thank you," to the gift giver (earthly or heavenly), but in my heart, I wanted to flee from them. It really wasn't them I wanted to flee from but a part of me that I didn't want to encounter. My heart screamed, "You are too insignificant to have this gift!" The Lord revealed to me that there was a level of love that needed to be unmasked. What part of God's love, His character, or His name needs to be uncovered? Out of sincerity, surrender to God to allow Him to position you to receive all of Him. Record your prayer.

2. Read Psalm 139. Focus on verses 17-18. Imagine an endless sandy beach (or go to a beach if you are near one). As you meditate on these verses, imagine if each grain of sand could speak a precious thought God has for you. The sum of these treasured thoughts, after trying to count them, would be endless, and yet God says His precious thoughts would be even *more* numerous than the sand grains. Thank Him for His boundless love.

3. Cultivate a designated time to meet with God for the sole purpose of practicing the presence of God whereby *He* is enjoying *your* presence. Hear Him call you who you are. You may use the verses in Appendix E to help you focus on His thoughts toward you and who you are to Him.

Let's Pray

Lord, You're too wonderful for our minds to comprehend Your precious thoughts towards us. They are more numerous than the grains of sand on the shore. Reveal our true identity through Your Scriptures and cause us to believe who You say we are. Forever grateful, Amen.

Let's Sing:

Sing along with my sister on piano by scanning the QR code or visit my website under "Hymns in My Book."

authordeborahrodriguez.com

A ROYAL IDENTITY

*M*y mind staggers to comprehend the vast chasm between my view of myself and God's view of me; my perceived insignificance versus my true significance and value. When I cleanse my mind with the truth, the breach gets more narrow by the day, and I'm learning to see myself the way God does. *"But when the fullness of the time had come, God sent forth His Son, born of a woman, born under the law, to redeem those who were under the law, that we might receive the adoption as sons [daughters]. And because you are sons [daughters], God has sent forth the Spirit of His Son into your hearts, crying out, 'Abba, Father!' Therefore, you are no longer a slave but a son [daughter], and if a son [daughter], then an heir of God through Christ"* (Galatians 4:4-7, brackets added). Are you a son (daughter) of God? An heir of God? If not, I want to invite you to understand the meaning of this most privileged relationship with the God of the universe through a relationship with Jesus Christ (See Appendix F).

My experience since receiving the gift of salvation through a relationship with Jesus Christ at a young age has been to make Jesus happy. I loved Jesus! I was one of those compliant kids who wanted to make Mom and Dad happy. I mostly kept the rules of the home, respected my teachers, shared the Gospel with my high school friends, but the concept of *thinking* like an heir of God through Christ Jesus was nonexistent. If I was adopted as a daughter of the King of Kings, no longer a slave to sin, and an heir of God through Christ Jesus, what was I lacking? I believe I was lacking a "kingdom" mentality; one of thinking like a King's kid—like royalty.

In the book of I Samuel, God established Saul's significance and called him to royalty, even though he was not from a royal lineage. However, Saul did not perceive his God-given worth. Perhaps you will see yourself in this Biblical example.

In I Samuel 9, Saul was asked to find his father's lost donkeys. After a long search, Saul tells his servant that they had better return home because his father may start worrying more about them than about the lost donkeys. His servant suggests asking an honorable man of God in another city where the donkeys are because all that the prophet says comes to pass. Saul agrees, and they go.

Meanwhile, God had already spoken to the prophet Samuel, telling him that Saul was going to come and that he should anoint Saul commander over His people Israel, *"'that he may save My people from the hand of the Philistines; for I have looked upon My people, because their cry has come to Me.' So, when Samuel detected Saul, the LORD said to him, 'There he is, the man of whom I spoke to you. This one shall reign over My people,'"* (I Samuel 9:16-17).

When they met, Saul inquired where the house of the prophet was. Samuel answered,

> *"'I am the seer. Go up before me to the high place, for you shall eat with me today; and tomorrow I will let you go and will tell you all that is*

in your heart. But as for your donkeys that were lost three days ago, do not be anxious about them, for they have been found. And on whom is all the desire of Israel? Is it not on you and on all your father's house?' And Saul answered and said, 'Am I not a Benjamite, of the smallest of the tribes of Israel, and my family the least of all the families of the tribe of Benjamin. Why then do you speak like this to me?' Now Samuel took Saul and his servant and brought them into the hall and had them sit in the place of honor among those who were invited; there were about thirty persons. And Samuel said to the cook, 'Bring the portion which I gave you of which I said to you, "Set it apart."' So the cook took up the thigh with its upper part and set it before Saul. And Samuel said, 'Here it is, what was kept back. It was set apart for you. Eat; for until this time it has been kept for you, since I said I invited the people.' So Saul ate with Samuel that day," (I Samuel 9:19-24).

The next day Saul and his servant departed, but before they went out of the city, Samuel told Saul to send his servant ahead of them. The prophet said to Saul, *"But you stand here awhile, that I may announce to you the word of God,"* (I Samuel 9:27b).

Wouldn't it astonish or bewilder you if a man of God said those things to you? I would think, *"I was just looking for Dad's donkeys and now this holy man of God wants to tell me over lunch what's in my heart. And what in the world does he mean that all the desire of my whole country is on me? I'm from the smallest tribe of Israel and my family is the least of all the families out of all the tribes. I don't think they even know I exist! He's got this all wrong. Why is he speaking to me like this?"* Samuel never answers that question, and the next thing you know, Saul is not only eating lunch with the highly esteemed prophet, but he is seated in the place of honor among 30 invited guests. Samuel graciously honors Saul by asking the cook to bring the best portion of food that was prepared and set aside just for Saul. Wouldn't you question, *"Hmmm, why am I being honored? And why did he set aside a special portion for me? He didn't know I was coming, did he? He doesn't even know me!"* Before Saul leaves the city, he hears the Word of God spoken by the prophet. Don't you think he was "all ears" after all he just experienced? By this time, I wondered what he was thinking!

The prophet highly valued him as royalty when Saul didn't envision himself as such. The prophet honored him above all others even though Saul saw himself as the smallest and the least. The prophet spoke—in front of others—of how unique and set apart the food was for Saul, compared to all the others. Saul had no expectation of the prophet's words or actions. Yet it doesn't stop there.

"Then Samuel took a flask of oil and poured it on his head, and kissed him and said: 'Is it not because the LORD has anointed you commander over His inheritance?'" (I Samuel 10:1). He wanted Saul to know that it was the Lord, not him, that anointed him commander over His inheritance. As we know now, Saul was to be king over Israel. Kingship conveys honor, nobility, majesty, royalty, power, influence, and authority. God, using Samuel as a conduit of His love, saw what was in Saul's heart while Saul saw none of it. The prophet called out what was there when Saul didn't have a clue.

The prophet continues to prophesy a series of events in Chapter 10 as confirmation of all that just took place, and finally, Samuel proclaims, *"Then the Spirit of the LORD will come upon you, and you will prophesy with them and be turned into another man,"* (I Samuel 10:6). That's what God does! He turns you into a new person when you see yourself as He does! Royalty! Blessed! Significant in God's sight! Prince! (Princess!)

Here is a breakdown of the rest of I Samuel 10:

✿　10:7: Samuel assures Saul that God is with Him.

Once God transforms you, He reassures He is with you. This may be through His Word, godly friends, authorities, life circumstances, or even nature—really, through anything He chooses.

✿　10:8-9: Samuel says he'll visit him in seven days and show him what he should do. The moment that Saul turns his back to go home, God gave him a different heart, and all the events that Samuel prophesied just moments before came to pass that day.

The God of all creation is not just with you, but dwells within you in all His names! (See Appendix B) He will show you what to do, and He will give you another heart, a heart like His. This new heart is fertile ground for the Spirit of God, ready for Him to use, to empower you to use the talents and gifts He created you with the day He fearfully and wonderfully made you.

✿　10:10-16: Saul meets a group of prophets, then the Spirit of God comes upon him, and he prophecies. All those who formerly knew him were amazed at the difference in his life. They wondered what came over him. Saul's uncle inquires about his journey to find the donkeys and what the prophet said to him. Saul only reveals the prophet said that the donkeys were found. He doesn't disclose all the other happenings.

Living in this place of victory will cause those around you who knew you before to ask, "What is this that has come on him (her)?" Just as Saul's uncle questioned him after all of this, we too will be questioned, even doubted—maybe misunderstood. Saul was wise in choosing who to tell his experience to and who not to. Interestingly, he chose not to tell a family member.

✿ 10:16-24: Samuel gathers the children of Israel together before the LORD and reveals Saul as their king since they rejected God as King. When they looked for Saul, he couldn't be found. In fact, they had to inquire of the LORD whether he was there. The Lord told them where he was—hiding among the baggage. They had to run and bring him out to be presented to all the people. Samuel says to the people, "Do you see him whom the LORD has chosen, that there is no one like him among all the people?" The people shout, "Long live the king!" (v. 24)

You may want to hide in the "baggage" you've lived with for so long when this transformation takes place, but God's pursuing love will not let you go. He won't leave you in your comfort zone. God will orchestrate life to bring you out of your baggage, and when He does, you will give Him the glory for standing a head taller. The *Lord* chose you!

✿ 10:25: Samuel explains to the people the behavior of royalty. He wrote it in a book and laid it up before the LORD. Then the people went home.

Wouldn't you have just loved to be there when Samuel explained to the people the behavior of royalty or read from the book he recorded it in? I wonder if God wanted it recorded in a book so that if Saul needed a reminder of how to act like royalty, he could go back to the "Book of Royalty" to find out?

- Saul travels home, and valiant men went with him, whose hearts God had touched. But some rebels said, "How can this man save us?" and despised him.

When Saul went home, some courageous men went with him, men whose hearts God had moved, but there were also rebels who despised Saul and questioned how he could save them. Declaring Saul as king just didn't make sense to the rebels. Royalty doesn't hide in the baggage. But God saw him differently. He sees you differently too! There will be those whose hearts will be touched by how God is working in your life, and there will be those who question or even despise you as you learn how to walk in your God-given royalty. Walk in kingdom royalty anyway! Remember, the crown(s) He places on your head, you will conceivably cast at Jesus' nail-scarred feet. Glory be to God!

Saul set out merely to recover his father's donkeys but ended up becoming a royal king of a whole nation. He thought he was simply honoring his father, but God gave him much more. We can speculate that, in our loving obedience to our Heavenly Father, He desires to lavish His blessing on us. Small beginnings turn into royal purposes when we let God have His way in the circumstances of life.

I'm not implying that it is a guarantee that you will become rich, powerful, famous, or comfortable. But I am speaking to what God wants to do in your heart. He wants to make you rich in experiencing Him through His promises. He wants to make you powerful in His might to declare His truth and bring His kingdom of light to those around you. He wants His name to be famous in you first, and then He wants you to proclaim it to give hope to others in your sphere of influence. He wants you to prepare your heart as a comfortable dwelling place for Christ, knowing that your purity and identity found in Him affects your relationship with Him and your peace within.

We can see every moment as from Him, whether we're looking for our "donkeys," or feeling hopeless and overwhelmed. Have you ever lost something? Saul's father lost his donkeys, but look what it led to. His son was anointed to be king! God wants to crown us with blessings and rewards when we see His way and draw close to Him through trusting His name and every facet of His character.

What is He declaring through His name to you? Rest in El Roi—the God who sees. He sees you, not just physically, but where you're at mentally, emotionally, physically, and spiritually. He is Provider—Jehovah Jireh, and when He comes through for you, He gets all the glory, honor, and praise! This is the adventurous life of having faith in the One who created you and loves you without end!

Just as loving, responsible parents want to give good gifts and rewards to their children, so too does Christ. He truly delights in those who delight in Him, and of course, delighting in Him means to love what He loves and hate what He hates. It's a two-way street. When we surrender to His love and instruction, we see *His* delight in us:

> ✿ *"The LORD your God in your midst, The Mighty One, will save; He will rejoice over you with gladness, He will quiet you with His love, He will rejoice over you with singing"* (Zephaniah 3:17).

✣ *"The LORD takes pleasure in those who fear Him, in those who hope in His mercy"* (Psalm 147:11).

And we gladly overflow with *our* delight in Him...

✣ *"Delight yourself also in the LORD, and He shall give you the desires of your heart"* (Psalm 37:4).

✣ *"Let all those who seek You rejoice and be glad in You; and let those who love Your salvation say continually, 'Let God be magnified!'"* (Psalm 70:4).

Most of my Christian life was focused on how I could show my love to God without expectation of any reward from Him because He had given me so much already. But now, His Word is alive in areas to which I gave little thought regarding His pleasure in rewarding me.   Let's see what He says Himself. Ponder each promise from the Bible. The emphasis in these verses is mine:

✣ *"Indeed the LORD has proclaimed to the end of the world: 'Say to the daughter of Zion, "Surely your salvation is coming; behold, His **reward** is with Him, and His work before Him."' And they shall call them The Holy People, The Redeemed of the LORD; And you shall be called Sought Out, A City Not Forsaken"* (Isaiah 62:11-12).

✣ *"And behold, I am coming quickly, and My **reward** is with Me, to give to everyone according to his work. I am the Alpha and the Omega, the Beginning and the End, the First and the Last."*

✣ *"**Blessed** are those who do His commandments, that they may have the right to the tree of life, and may enter through the gates into the city"* (Revelation 22:12-14).

❀ *"...Refrain your voice from weeping, And your eyes from tears; for your work shall be* **rewarded***, says the LORD, And they shall come back from the land of the enemy. There is hope in your future, says the LORD, that your children shall come back to their own border"* (Jeremiah 31:16-17).

❀ *"But you, when you pray, go into your room, and when you have shut your door, pray to your Father who is in the secret place; and your Father who sees in secret will* **reward** *you openly"* (Matthew 6:6).

❀ *"And whoever gives one of these little ones only a cup of cold water in the name of a disciple, assuredly, I say to you, he shall by no means lose his* **reward***"* (Matthew 10:42).

❀ *"The wicked man does deceptive work, but he who sows righteousness will have a sure* **reward***"* (Proverbs 11:18).

❀ *"Behold, the Lord GOD shall come with a strong hand, and His arm shall rule for Him; Behold, His* **reward** *is with Him, and His work before Him"* (Isaiah 40:10).

❀ *"But love your enemies, do good, and lend, hoping for nothing in return; and your* **reward** *will be great, and you will be sons of the Most High. For He is kind to the unthankful and evil"* (Luke 6:35).

❀ *"...Do not be afraid, Abram. I am your shield, your exceedingly great* **reward***"* (Genesis 15:1).

The last one is a clincher. God. *Is.* My. Exceedingly. Great. Reward. His matchless name cannot be grasped in our limited earthly comprehension, yet He pursues us to reveal more and more of Himself at even deeper levels of understanding and intimacy! This is who lives in us to enable us! Thank you, Jesus!

As if rewards are not enough to be humbled by, there are crowns which He will bestow when we see His face:

- ✿ The Crown of Righteousness: *"Finally, there is laid up for me the crown of righteousness, which the Lord, the righteous Judge, will give to me on that Day, and not to me only but also to all who have longed for His appearing"* (2 Timothy 4:8).

- ✿ The Crown of Life: *"Blessed is the man who endures temptation; for when he has been approved, he will receive the crown of life which the Lord has promised to those who love Him"* (James 1:12).

- ✿ The Crown of Glory: *"Shepherd the flock of God which is among you, serving as overseers, not by compulsion but willingly, not for dishonest gain but eagerly; nor as being lords over those entrusted to you, but being examples to the flock; and when the Chief Shepherd appears, you will receive the crown of glory that does not fade away"* (1 Peter 5:2-4).

Clearly, our motive for walking with Christ on earth is not merely to gain a crown in heaven, or earn rewards. For you see, HE is our exceedingly great reward. HE is our "crown." There is no glorious crown that will compare to the sight and presence of our Lord and Savior Jesus Christ! Any crown or reward He imparts is merely one that He enabled us to receive. It is only His all-consuming grace and mercy that qualifies and empowers us to operate in this kingdom of light: *"Christ in you, the hope of glory"* (Colossians 1:27). Out of heartfelt gratitude and true worship, we will not only receive a crown(s) from His nail-scarred hands, but we will also cast our crowns at His nail-scarred feet knowing, experiencing, honoring, and praising the One who is worthy of every tear, question, trial, or suffering. *"Eye has not seen, nor ear heard, nor have entered into the heart of man the things which God has prepared for those who love Him"* (1 Corinthians 2:9). Hallelujah! *"Behold, I am coming quickly! Hold fast what you have, that no one may take your crown"* (Revelation 3:11).

Just as God groomed Saul for royalty, He does the same for us. He sees who we really are. Once we receive the blessing of knowing God personally through a relationship with Jesus Christ, we need to see ourselves the way God sees us. Receiving the truth about who we are in Christ transforms our mind. As it transforms our mind, it transforms our behavior to be more like Him. Soon, the feelings of royalty emerge.

God's heart resonated with mine in a way that caused me to face the reality of how my lack of royal thinking in the past affected my sphere of influence. Sometimes reality hurts. That reality transformed how I saw my relationships.

Key Take-Aways:

✦ God transforms us into royalty when we become His child, but we need to have a kingdom mentality and choose to see ourselves as Christ does.

✦ The God of all creation is not just with you but dwells within you in all His names.

✦ Small beginnings turn into royal purposes when we allow God to have His way in the everyday circumstances in life.

✦ Out of heartfelt gratitude and true worship, we will not only receive a crown by His nail-scarred hands but also cast our crowns at His nail-scarred feet, knowing, experiencing, honoring, and praising the One who is worthy of every tear, question, trial, or suffering.

✦ **God** *is* our exceedingly Great Reward.

Let's Reflect:

1. Do you perceive yourself as a pauper or a prince(ss) in the kingdom of God? Just as you thirst for a cold drink of water on a hot day, develop a thirst for the truth that Jesus delights in you. You are a child of the King. *"Wherefore thou art no more a servant, but a son; and if a son, then an heir of God through Christ"* (Galatians 4:7). As an heir of God, what comes to your mind? What does this mean? Jot down or draw what you think or feel.

2. Having peace with God through a loving relationship with Jesus Christ is the greatest gift of all. If you haven't already received the Gift of all gifts—Jesus Christ, through the forgiveness of sin, and the gift of eternal life, ask Him (See Appendix F). Maybe you are sensing a need to recommit your life to Him. If there is an aspect of truth out of balance about who Jesus Christ is and His character, ask Him to reveal Himself to you as you diligently seek Him. Journal your prayer.

3. As a devoted follower of Christ, embrace who He calls you. Read Appendix E: Who God Calls You. Spend time meditating on each of these verses over time, asking God to reveal your true identity and experience Him. Create a personal list of the traits that jump out at you and pen what God is saying to you through it.

Let's Pray:

O Lord, our mind reels when we meditate on how You are delighted when we cry, "Abba (daddy), Father." As a good Father, You call us children of the King of Kings if we choose to let You live and reign in our hearts. Thank You! Groom us for royalty, for that is what we are because You said so. In that grooming, may we believe most of all, along with Abram, that *You* are our exceeding great Reward! *"Blessed be the God and Father of our Lord Jesus Christ, who has blessed us with every spiritual blessing in the heavenly places in Christ"* (Ephesians 1:3). In Jesus' name, Amen.

Let's Sing:

Sing along with my sister on piano by scanning the QR code or visit my website under "Hymns in My Book."

authordeborahrodriguez.com

REALITY

*A*s the pendulum swung from one extreme to another, God allowed me to experience the pain I had caused others. Each life experience in learning who I am and Whose I am was orchestrated out of God's loving, tender mercy and faithfulness. But now He allowed me to walk, in a very limited way, in the shoes of those who were the recipients of my life lived with the truth out of balance. I felt the pain I inflicted on loved ones through harsh words, anger, frustration, and confusion, which resulted in walls in our relationship. This brought me to a place of crying out to God to be forgiven and seeking forgiveness from those I hurt.

False humility, like fallow ground, was dug up by my Faithful Redeemer and He exposed the deep, dark side of the entangled root of pride in the depths of my soul. His tender love, beyond measure, revealed that when I believe who I say I am, then I am not believing who God says I am. I set myself up as God when I believe me, instead of Him. I. Am. Not. God.

Just as a toddler falls repeatedly when learning how to walk, I too did the same as I learned how to live like a royal child of the King. My sister always rolls out the red carpet for me when I visit. The first morning I woke up after flying in, she handed me a tea cup that said, "God Bless Your Beautiful Spirit." My immediate thought was, "That sure isn't me." A few days later, while we sat at the dinner table, a decorative

Jello mold hanging from her kitchen wall fell to the floor with a tinny clang. Our heads jerked in the direction of the clatter. My conclusion was, "It's my fault. I was the last one in the kitchen." Two "minor" things spoke in a "major" way. Because of the redeeming work of Christ, I was able to discern where those thoughts came from... the accuser.

In some areas, I still feel as though I'm walking in step with a toddler, and yet in other areas, I feel like I have been running a marathon. I'm so glad for God's never-ending patience, especially in times when others see the toddler in me. I'm thankful for the blood of Jesus, who washed my sins away and purified my heart. I'm grateful that I can learn from my past and not permit it to define me or control me—there is too much at stake to allow that to continue to happen. With praise on my lips for what He has done, and for His forgiveness, I can have a heart that is not burdened by guilt, *"being confident of this very thing, that He who has begun a good work in you [me] will complete it until the day of Jesus Christ"* (Philippians 1:6, brackets added). He's not done with me yet! Just as Saul learned how to live a life of royalty, we too can be delivered from "hiding out in the baggage" of our past and live like a son/daughter of the King. From Genesis to Revelation, it tells us of our identity. As we meditate and rehearse these truths that identify us, our thinking will transform, our feelings will begin to line up to the truth, which in turn, changes our behavior to reflect Whose we are. Here are truths we can receive about who we are and what is ours in Christ:

✿ We are God's handiwork:

"For we are His workmanship, created in Christ Jesus for good works, which God prepared beforehand that we should walk in them" (Ephesians 2:10).

✿ We are children of God:

"But as many as received Him, to them He gave the right to become children of God, to those who believe in His name" (John 1:12).

✿ We are overcomers:

"You are of God, little children, and have overcome them, because He who is in you is greater than he who is in the world" (1 John 4:4).

✿ We are friends of Jesus:

"No longer do I call you servants, for a servant does not know what his master is doing; but I have called you friends, for all things that I heard from My Father I have made known to you" (John 15:15).

✿ We receive God's power, love, and a sound mind:

"For God has not given us a spirit of fear, but of power and of love and of a sound mind" (2 Timothy 1:7).

✿ We receive mercy and find grace to help in time of need:

"Let us therefore come boldly to the throne of grace, that we may obtain mercy and find grace to help in time of need" (Hebrews 4:16).

✿ We receive forgiveness and cleansing of sin:

"If we confess our sins, He is faithful and just to forgive us our sins and to cleanse us from all unrighteousness" (I John 1:9).

* We have received a gift from God to serve one another:

  "As each one has received a gift, minister it to one another, as good stewards of the manifold grace of God" (1 Peter 4:10).

* We have been delivered from the kingdom of darkness:

  "He has delivered us from the power of darkness and conveyed us into the kingdom of the Son of His love" (Colossians 1:13).

* We are fearfully and wonderfully made:

  "I will praise You, for I am fearfully and wonderfully made; Marvelous are Your works, and that my soul knows very well" (Psalm 139:14).

* We receive the mind of Christ:

  "For 'who has known the mind of the LORD that he may instruct Him?' But we have the mind of Christ" (1 Corinthians 2:16).

* We receive a hope and a future:

  "For I know the thoughts that I think toward you, says the LORD, thoughts of peace and not of evil, to give you a future and a hope" (Jeremiah 29:11).

* We are supplied all our needs:

  "And my God shall supply all your needs according to His riches in glory by Christ Jesus" (Philippians 4:19).

The list of who God calls you and what He wants us to receive as we walk by faith goes on and on. I have given more references in Appendix E. If we truly begin to believe we are who God calls us, we can be sure that there will be a battle between the kingdom of darkness and the kingdom of light for our identity. Satan will also attack our minds with lies so that we will not experience freedom from wrong thinking. We must wash our minds with the truth of God's Word and trust God in the process. Then, after a time, we can look back and see that our thoughts which once caused us worry, rejection, anger, or shame, are now transformed to trust that we are more than conquerors through Christ Jesus. The times we run will outnumber the times we fall.

When I look into the rearview mirror of life, I see how I was continuously taking my spiritual pulse. Nothing is wrong with checking our spiritual heart rate and rhythm to see if it pulsates with our Savior's. Making sure we are doing all the right things—being responsible, committed, observing His commands, putting a smile on His face, is what we long to do when we love Him. However, there was now a divine unveiling. I realized that when we continually take our spiritual pulse, constantly asking, "How am *I* doing?" "Do *I* line up to God?" "Am *I* obeying His commands?" We are still focused on ourselves. It is as if we are leaning on our ability instead of His ability in us. When our eyes are fixed on our Lord and Savior Jesus Christ (in all of who He is through His names), *He* becomes enthroned in our hearts *"to will and to do for His good pleasure"* (Philippians 2:13). He is our Enabler, and He is All-Sufficient. We can be dangerously out of balance when we are focused on one more than the other.

This concept reminds me of the time my youngest daughter needed an MRI at age three because of her bone issues. We came equipped with her favorite Bible song CD as an encouraging diversion to listen to when the drumming of the long scan began. The technicians positioned her on the MRI bed, placed the headphones on her head, and in she went. I was able to hold her hand through the entire test, and I prayed she would not be fearful and remain motionless. With her eyes fixed on mine and mine on hers literally the entire 45 minutes, she was calm and peaceful. She knew she was okay because she sensed in my countenance and spirit that I was at peace. She took on my likeness (which was completely Jehovah-Shalom—The Lord My Peace). As we behold our God above, we will become like the One we behold.

The Lord My Peace who dwelt in me was the power in ministering to my daughter. Acknowledging the names of Christ/God who lives in our heart can be practiced in our everyday life.

Functioning in life from abundance can expose painful places in our heart where we lived in lack. It takes time and patience with ourselves and beholding the God of faithfulness to grasp the new way of thinking. It's a journey, not a destination.

Key Take-Aways:

+ God may allow us to experience the pain we've caused when we were living out of lack instead of abundance, but we need to receive the gift of forgiveness for sin through the blood of Jesus and continue to ask Him to purify our hearts.
+ Our past does not have to define us or control us.
+ God began a good work in us, and He will complete it until the day we see Him.
+ We become like the One we behold.

Let's Reflect:

1. As God brings to mind the heartache we brought to the lives of our loved ones from living our lives out of lack instead of abundance, we can be overwhelmed. Read Philippians 1:6. We can be confident through the finished work of Christ on the cross that the good work God began in us will also be completed. Receive His gift of forgiveness and trust Him to finish the work in you. Then, with a repentant heart, go to those you have hurt and allow God to bring reconciliation. Leave the results in His hands. Make a list of people. Pray for an opportunity. Trust Him. Rest.

2. Our past does not define us or control us. In Philippians 3:13-14, Paul claims he is not perfect, but he presses on: *"forgetting those things which are behind and reaching forward to those things which are ahead... the goal for the prize of the upward call of God in Christ Jesus."* Create a sacred place in your heart and mind and lay your past at His feet, not forgetting the lessons learned from it, but consecrating your life to a new beginning in the newfound truths you have learned. Commit and formulate your prayer as you respond to Him.

3. As we "put on" our identity in Christ and appropriate His names, at times we will be in places and with people who need to experience Him. Pray for opportunities to be a conduit of His Spirit and reach out to these individuals. Record the results of these encounters for future reference. On days you need to be encouraged and remember God's faithfulness, you can read these stories. In case you need help

embracing who lives in you in your identity, find Appendix B and C for the Names of God and Names of Jesus.

Let's Pray:

Lord, you have begun a good work in me, and you promised to complete it. I thank you that by Your grace, and through faith, I trust I am empowered by your Holy Spirit to victoriously...

...reach the broken from my own brokenness.

...unmask my weakness as a megaphone of Your strength.

...proclaim truth from my experience with the Truth Giver to magnify Your name.

...reveal my healing wounds to bring healing to the wounds of others.

...expose my scars as a mark of beauty to those who wear their hidden scars hoping to someday shout *their* story of redemption to those who need to hear it. Then to point to the One whose scarred hands redeemed them.

...manifest the wounded soldier in me to roar as a lion to proclaim He is worthy to be honored and praised to a world that wants to hide or deny their wounds.

May our brokenness, our wounds, and our scars shout with the all-sufficiency of Christ (through all His Names) in every aspect of life.

You have promised the comforts for which You comforted us will be the comfort which we give one another (2 Corinthians 1:4).

You are worthy! We are of great worth because of You! In Jesus' name, Amen!

Let's Sing:

Sing along with my sister on piano by scanning the QR code or visit my website under "Hymns in My Book."

authordeborahrodriguez.com

OPERATING OUT OF
ABUNDANCE

*W*hat God proclaims is what is true. Functioning in life as a wife, mother, home-schooling mom, pastor's wife, daughter in my "new" relationship to Dad, sister, and friend took on new meaning. There was a deeper level of confidence in God that came naturally.

With newfound eyes I became more alert for opportunities to receive from God as He revealed Himself. I saw each obstacle, challenge, and decision as an experience to cry out and experience Him in His name. Whether it was a business, legal, or health encounter for my dad, how to deal with educational challenges for my kids, braving church decisions, tackling relational challenges in the home, or just life in general, my soul responded from a more peaceful, joy-filled framework. The focus no longer was, "What can I do for you, God?" but "God, through your enablement of who You are in me, what do You want to do? And if you choose, use me!"

This was a peaceful, restful place to dwell—in His power and might. I imagined myself as a poor, destitute beggar. Hungry. Skin and bones. Wearing dirty, tattered clothes. Empty; impoverished of any gift or talent mentally, emotionally, spiritually, or materially. Utterly dependent on

His mind, His Spirit, His provision: *"Christ in me, the hope of glory"* (Colossians 1:27). In my weakness, I was positioned to be strong in Him. All our striving ceases as we abide in Him, knowing that He is sovereign and in control. Peace and joy (or the lack thereof) became my spiritual barometer for my trust in God. When fear or anxiety arose, I was quickened in my spirit to protect that place of rest in my soul. So, fear and anxiety became a springboard to cast my cares on the All-Sufficient One. Sometimes—no, many times-throughout the day.

Trials, challenges, and decisions became opportunities to experience God in His name at every turn. I looked for it. If peace with God was in the least bit compromised, I knew I was not trusting in the One who healed and pursued me. If there was anything or anyone who I allowed to steal my joy that was now so full, I wrestled until I got it back through prayer, repentance, or proclaiming God's promises. This did not negate feelings of sadness, discouragement, anger, loneliness, overwhelming odds, or rejection, but these feelings became immediate springboards of seeking God as the One who is the Great I AM, the All-Sufficient One. Second Corinthians 12:9 affirms: *"And He said to me, 'My grace is sufficient for you, for My strength is made perfect in weakness.' Therefore most gladly I will rather boast in my infirmities, that the power of Christ may rest upon me."* Our royal identity as heirs of the Creator of the universe is no small thing! His power rests on us. And in us.

The treasure of experiencing God through His names became more exciting to me than the weight of the trial I was experiencing. Life was an adventure, not knowing what it held but knowing Who held me tightly in His hands. The weight shifted from me holding tightly to God's hand (which is imperative), to Him having a grip on me that was fiercer and more fervent than mine could ever be. I imagined it was like I was drowning in a turbulent ocean of helplessness, flailing my arms as if to rescue myself from the grips of death. While thrashing and floundering in the tumultuous waters, the Lover of My Soul reached out and exclaimed, "Take my hand!" He didn't say, "Give me your hand!" What's the difference between those statements? When you're drowning, you are at the mercy of the one who is rescuing you. You have absolutely nothing to give. You need to *take* the rescuer's hand in order to live. Christ came to grasp our hand (life) and rescue us from our sin and self to grant us life abundant. We have nothing to give in and of ourselves except our broken life. He pursues. He rescues. He saves.

How does that look practically? We need to recognize our need for Him, revealed to us by the Holy Spirit. We may need forgiveness of sin, deliverance from strongholds, comfort for our wounded soul, strength for our journey, wisdom for decisions, or anything else. At times we will know what we have need of, and at other times we may not because of a blind spot, stronghold, pride, deep unknown woundedness, or lies we have believed. In God's faithfulness and because of His pursuing love, He reveals what we have need of. Perhaps the depths of His love has not yet been experienced because we haven't relinquished our lives to Him. I implore you to surrender to Him (see Appendix F).

When we surrender to what He allows, as difficult as it may be, it can turn into peace, joy, and a more profound understanding of His lavished love on His treasured children. *"But He knows the way that I take; when He has tested me, I will come forth as gold"* (Job 23:10). *"And He said to me, 'My grace is sufficient for you, for My strength is made perfect in weakness.' Therefore most gladly I will rather boast in my infirmities, that the power of Christ may rest upon me"* (2 Corinthians 12:9). That power comes in trusting in His Name (character). In practical terms, we can shift our thinking to this:

- ✿ If we didn't need healing, we wouldn't need Jehovah Raphe—the LORD who Heals.

- ✿ If we didn't need His provision (materially, mentally, emotionally, physically, spiritually) we wouldn't need Jehovah Jireh—the LORD my Provider.

- ✿ If we didn't need someone to defend us, we wouldn't need Jehovah Maginnenu— the LORD my Defense.

- ✿ If we didn't need mercy, then we wouldn't need Elohim Chaseddi—God of my Mercy.

- ✿ If we didn't need His mighty power and strength, then we wouldn't need Jehovah El Elohim—LORD God of Gods, Mighty, Powerful, Strong One over All.

- ✿ If we didn't need His help, then we wouldn't need Elohim Ozer Li—God my Helper.

- ✿ If we didn't need to know the truth, then we wouldn't need Jehovah El Emeth—the LORD God of Truth.

- ✿ If we didn't need to be made pure and holy, then we wouldn't need Jehovah Mekoddishkem—the LORD Who Sanctifies You, Makes Holy.

- ✿ If we didn't need peace, we wouldn't need Jehovah Shalom—the LORD is Peace.

BUT WE DO NEED HIM!

We desperately need Him! He is the great *"I Am That I Am,"* (Exodus 3:14, KJV)—God, manifest in all His names. So, we can gladly say, "Lord, thank you that I have a need for peace in the midst of the storm I'm facing. I'm desperate, but if I didn't have this storm I wouldn't have the opportunity to experience You as the great 'I AM' who wants to reveal Yourself to me as Jehovah-Shalom—the Lord is Peace."

When my youngest daughter was facing her ninth surgery, I prayed as usual for her healing. This time, however, I had a new level of trust in our Almighty God, asking Him to be true to His name as Jehovah Rapha—the Lord that Heals (Exodus 15:26, Jeremiah 33:6, Isaiah 30:26, 61:1, Psalm 103:3). Peace and confidence in Christ surpassed my worry and anxiety. He was Jehovah Shalom—the Lord my Peace.

Overwhelmed with life one day, I entreated Him with a heavy heart, "God, don't you see what's happening? Don't you see?" It was said, not in an angry way, but a plea to intervene about the situation. As I stared out the dining room window pondering this, I looked up into the heavens and saw a perfectly crafted eyebrow and eye fashioned out of the clouds, including eyelids, iris, and pupils. Unmistakably, His answer was, "Yes, I see you, Deborah." It wasn't a trite, "Yes, I see with my physical eyes." It was deep calling to deep, penetrating the longings of my heart and ministering to my spirit. He was at work even though I could not discern with my earthly eyes. I wept as His wondrous love washed over my soul. He took the time to create an answer just for me! El Roi revealed Himself to me. Yes, El Roi—The God That Sees Me, sees you (Genesis 16:13).

Another reality of His name I experienced was Jehovah Rah—The Lord My Shepherd. Once a daughter who knew little about my dad's private life, and now needing to know all the details, I was overwhelmed. Engulfed by new, and many times difficult to understand, information, I needed God to be my Jehovah Rah. As a shepherd guides, leads, and comforts, I craved this from Him. My prayers changed from, "God, I need your direction and comfort" to "God *be* my direction and comfort; *be* my Jehovah Rah." I grew to desire *Him* more than His help; desiring the Gift-Giver more than the gift. He became a nearer and dearer friend.

There are many more names of God that He proved to be true by experience in my life. He has been my Jehovah Gibbor-Milchaman—the LORD Mighty in Battle (Psalm 24:8), El Shaddai—All-Sufficient One (Genesis 17:1), Jehovah Goelekh—the Lord my Redeemer (Isaiah 60:16), Jehovah Jireh—The Lord My Provider (Genesis 22:14), Jehovah Shamma—The Lord is There (Ezekiel 48:35), and many more. (See Appendix B)

I possessed a treasury in appropriating God's names and seeking Him through His Word in a new way. I didn't know I had this treasure at this level until it was unearthed by Him. God once again used the megaphone of my car to drive home a truth—no pun intended. My car needed to be towed on Thanksgiving Day because one of the cylinders had a burnt valve, which caused other problems of which I have no understanding. I had grown to expect great lessons from God through His gift of love, my car. I wasn't too bent out of shape about the situation, although I was a little disappointed to miss Thanksgiving celebrations with my husband's side of the family.

Ten days later, I picked up my car from the dealership with a new engine at no charge—it was supposed to be a $6,000 job! The serviceman had done his homework and found that the extended service warranty on my car covered the whole bill! Embarrassed that I didn't know the warranty would cover the cost, I asked for a printout of what the warranty included for future purposes. When he handed me the two-page, fine print list of coverage, once again tears welled up in my eyes. God began to speak to my heart, "Deborah, just as you didn't know the detailed benefits of your warranty, you will never know the riches of experiencing Me through the treasures of the promises of My Word if you don't dig deeper."

Feeling like everybody saw and heard what God just said to me, I shifted my eyes back and forth to see who was watching. I quickly folded those pages, stuffed them in my purse, and wiped the tears away. I was in awe once again of how God speaks to me through a car of which I have little mechanical knowledge. Once again, His pursuing love!

Operating in life from abundance instead of lack was a new paradigm. Knowing God at a deeper level through His names and promises of blessings brought a new trust in who He is. He shared His secrets with me and our bond was even closer. It's true that the *Lord is the portion of my inheritance and of my cup: He maintains my lot"* (Psalm 16:5). Since that day I committed to sincerely praying that prayer of Jabez, *"Oh, that You would bless me indeed, and enlarge my territory, that Your hand would be with me, and that You would keep me from evil, that I may not cause pain!"* (I Chronicles 4:10), I can wholeheartedly say that I would have never asked for the hurdles and complexities that God allowed in my life, but the treasure, blessing, and reward of experiencing Him far surpasses the trials. I'm so thankful God removed the veil from my heart and revealed the truth to bring me to higher ground and a deeper intimacy with Him. I'm delivered from insignificance and learning to embrace my royal identity in Christ. *He truly is my Reward!*

Recognizing the opportunity in every difficulty to become more intimate with our Lord and Savior Jesus Christ is a blessing that will bring ceaseless peace and rest when you acknowledge Him. *"Be still and know that I am God; ...The LORD of hosts is with us; The God of Jacob is our refuge. Selah"* (Psalm 46:10-11). We look for the opportunity. We expect the opportunity. We thank Him for the opportunity. Cleaving to Him and practicing the acknowledgement of His presence changes our thinking, feelings and actions. Even in the little things in life.

I was soon to learn that something as simple as what I wore could symbolize my deliverance from insignificance.

Key Take-Aways:

✦ Every decision, challenge, obstacle, or trial is an opportunity to experience God through His names when we cry out to Him.

✦ Who God is inside of us (through His names) enables us to be His conduit if we surrender our life to God.

✦ All our striving ceases as we abide in Christ.

✦ Peace and joy, or the lack thereof, become our spiritual barometer for our trust in God (through all His names).

✦ Fear and anxiety become a springboard to cast all our cares on the All-Sufficient One.

✦ Don't let anyone or anything steal your joy in the Lord. Wrestle until you get it back through prayer, repentance, or proclaiming the truth of God's promises.

✦ The treasure of experiencing God through His names outweighs the burden of any trial.

✦ When we surrender to what God allows, no matter how overwhelming it is, it can turn into peace, joy, and a more profound understanding of His lavished love if we ask Him to be who He says He is (through His names).

✦ Desire the Gift-Giver more than the gift.

✦ We will never know the riches of experiencing Christ through the treasures of the promises of God's Word if we don't dig deeper into His Word and experientially know His Wonderful Names.

Let's Reflect:

1. Read Colossians 1:27. Prayerfully ask God the meaning of *"Christ in me, the hope of glory."* Ask Him to reveal to you the difference between doing His will in *your* strength and doing His will with *His* grace and power. Record it in your journal.

2. How is your peace and joy barometer reading? If Christ can be trusted wholeheartedly, we can use our anxieties, worries, and fears as a springboard to ask Him by faith to cast them out, for *"perfect love casts out fear..."* (I John 4:18). Trade in your anxiety and fear for peace and joy in Christ by crying out to Him through His names. You may have to do it multiple times a day. Draw a line down the middle of your journal page. List the fears and anxieties or praises in your life on one side of the line, and on the other side write the name of God who is yearning to engage in a relationship with you. For example, on the left side of your journal page you can say, "Lord, my mind wants to race in anxiety about the possibility of losing my

job." On the right side of your journal page you can write, "Jehovah Shalom (God my Peace)-thank you I have the opportunity to cling to you through this uncertain time and experience you in a way that will bring me closer in relationship to you. I look to you to be my Peace."

3. Look in Appendix B. What name of God can you place in this prayer? "Lord, thank you that I have a need for (name your need)_____. I'm desperate and cry out to you. If I didn't have this storm (need), I wouldn't have the opportunity to experience You as (name of God) _____.
I trust you more than I seek an answer. I desire a relationship with You more than I desire You to fix my problem because I want to intimately know You."

Here is another sample: "Lord, I don't know what to do. I have no experience or knowledge in this difficult decision. I'm desperate and cry out to you. I thank you that I have this need for guidance and wisdom because if I didn't have this storm (need), I wouldn't have the opportunity to experience You as El De'ot (God of All Knowledge). I trust you and your unfailing love more than I seek the answer. I desire to draw near to you more than I desire You to fix my problem. Thank you for your loving care to reveal yourself to me. You are so good. In Jesus name, Amen."

Let's Pray:

Lord, I can't think of a better way to pray than to agree with Paul in his prayer, *"For this reason I bow my knees to the Father of our Lord Jesus Christ, from whom the whole family in heaven and earth is named, that He would grant you, according to the riches of His glory, to be strengthened with might through His Spirit in the inner man, that Christ may dwell in your hearts through faith; that you, being rooted and grounded in love, may be able to comprehend with all the saints what is the width and length and depth and height— to know the love of Christ which passes knowledge; that you may be filled with all the fullness of God. Now to Him who is able to do exceedingly abundantly above all that we ask or think, according to the power that works in us, to Him be glory in the church by Christ Jesus to all generations, forever and ever"* (Ephesians 3:14-21). In Jesus' name, Amen.

Let's Sing:

Sing along with my sister on piano by scanning the QR code or visit my website under "Hymns in My Book."

authordeborahrodriguez.com

CONCLUSION

OR MAYBE JUST THE BEGINNING

*I*t's been a while since I had that life-changing summer. Today, I woke up looking forward to worshiping with God's people. As I scanned my wardrobe, I picked out a short-sleeved, white peasant top with tiny, royal blue designs. I sensed God saying to me, "You've come a long way, Deborah." God reminded me of the day I bought that special blouse. After my dad was released from being supervised 24/7 and I was free to visit my family for a few hours in the evening, I sheepishly asked God, "Can I stop at K-Mart and buy something for myself? Is it selfish, Lord, to think of myself when Dad and my family need me? Should I take time out for myself when there are so many needs?" The Lord gave me the clearance to shop at K-Mart, and I purchased that short-sleeved, white peasant top with tiny royal blue designs to match my royal blue skirt. For some reason, it felt like a special gift from God to buy a blouse that God approved, even though needs surrounded me at my home and Dad's home. Yet, guilt won that day after I bought it because it felt self-centered.

After my healing, I wore that short-sleeved, white peasant top with joy, knowing that God delights in refreshing my soul and giving me good gifts. *"If you then, being evil, know how to give good gifts to your children, how much more will your Father who is in heaven give good things to those who ask Him"* (Matthew 7:11). Today, I wear that peasant blouse with confidence as a symbol and a reminder of how I need to live my life operating from an abundance mentality. He is a rewarder of those who diligently seek Him.

God has brought my dad miraculously far. As we were driving in my car that I call a "hug" from God, my dad related an observation. With a smile, he recognized that I've gained knowledge of things relating to his life. He was right. I've acquired wisdom in:

- Getting a reduced-fare bus pass
- Driving on highways that I had never traveled before to get to doctors and medical tests
- What it means to be a responsible power of attorney for healthcare and finances
- Making countless decisions regarding banking and business transactions
- How to deal with Medicare
- How to compare retirement communities for the best living conditions for your dollar
- How to deal with doctors and medical personnel from a patient's perspective
- How to communicate to a person dealing with aphasia
- Learning about community resources for senior citizens

Shall I go on?

Filled with gratitude and a heart of joy, I smiled back at Dad and said, "Because of you, I have the blessing of being more prepared to face my life as a senior citizen in the future." He nodded with a smile that seemed to say, "God is good, and His purposes are good." With a grateful heart, I recounted how God my Helper (Elohim Ozer Li) brought me through the valley to the mountain top, trusting and clinging even more to the One in whom *"we know that all things work together for good to those who love God, to those who are the called according to His purpose"* (Romans 8:28). He truly is a rewarder of those who diligently seek Him:

"But without faith it is impossible to please Him,
for he who comes to God must believe that He is,
and that He is a rewarder of those who diligently seek Him,"
(Hebrews 11:6)

I promise you, as sure as the promises of God, that as you surrender to God to reveal Himself through circumstances and trials in life, you will experience a richer, fuller, more abundant life than you have ever known. Intimacy with Christ is where our fulfillment and identity come from. We know who we are because of Whose we are. *He. Is. Our. Reward!*

We've all been to a wedding before. Picture a groom eagerly waiting for his cherished bride to emerge as the music signifies her approaching appearance. They have known each other in a somewhat limited sense until this special day. He has a burning in his eyes that communicates a fervent longing for his bride to be with him, right by his side forever, and to lay down his life for her. She, too, expectantly beholds her beloved, desiring him, lovingly responding to his desire and sacrificial love as their eyes meet. Passionate sacrificial love is mutual. Consummation of the relationship is near at hand.

Now, imagine Christ as our groom, and we as His bride. His passion for us far outweighs our desire for Him. He has longingly pursued His bride throughout the ages. We were on His mind long before we even had a thought of Him. While we were yet sinners, He gave His lifeblood so that we can have forgiveness of sin and intimacy with Him. We are the object of His abundant love. He, in every facet of His character in His name(s), is offered to us as we await consummation.

Christ is waiting to hear His Father's voice exclaim, "Jesus, go and get your bride." His anticipation to dwell with us in sweet intimacy is unimaginable because of His pursuing love for us to be with Him in perfect union forever. We will be caught up together with Him in the clouds to meet Him as He comes to take us away to be with Him forever, for He is Faithful and True (see I Thessalonians 4:17). His bride (believers) will be overjoyed and give Him glory, for the marriage of the Lamb has come and His bride has made herself ready. He will grant us to be arrayed in fine linen, clean and white, for the fine linens are our righteous acts. She is blessed who is called to the marriage supper of the Lamb! (see Revelation 19:7-9).

His eyes are like a flame of fire, and on His head are many crowns. He has a *name* written on Him that no one knows except Himself—I can't wait to see what that name is! He is clothed with a robe dipped in blood, and His name is called The Word of God (see Revelation 19:12-13). On His robe and thigh, a name is written: *King of Kings and Lord of Lords* (see Revelation 19:16). Our bridegroom will wipe away every tear from our eyes; there shall be no more death, nor sorrow, nor crying. There shall be no more pain, for the former things have passed away. He will make all things new and give of the fountain of the water of life freely to us because our name is in the Lamb's Book of Life (see Revelation 21:4-6). Imagine running into His arms as He runs toward you in anticipation of the consummation of your relationship. What a day that will be! To experience Him in His fullness... face to face... You, my friend, are worth it!

"Since we are surrounded by so great a cloud of witnesses, let us lay aside every weight, and the sin which so easily ensnares us, and let us run with endurance the race that is set before us, looking unto Jesus, the author and finisher of our faith, who for the joy that was set before Him endured the cross, despising the shame, and has sat down at the right hand of the throne of God" (Hebrews 12:1-2).

As we look unto Jesus, who endured the cross for us, our veil will be removed so we can behold and reflect the glory of the Lord. And the Spirit of the Lord makes us more and more like him, transforming us into His glorious image (see 2 Corinthians 3:18).

So, my new friend, my hope and prayer is that you will fill your heart up with the precious truth of God in His Word who calls you who you are. Cry out to Him in His name(s), then go out to a world that is on the other side of your trials and suffering, just waiting to hear the powerful message God has written on your heart because you trusted God to keep His promises. He is worthy! And He delights in you!

Key Take-Aways:

✦ God is Rewarder of those who diligently seek Him.

✦ God delights in refreshing our soul.

✦ As you surrender to God to reveal Himself through circumstances and trials in life, you will experience a richer, fuller, more abundant life than you have ever known.

✦ Intimacy with Christ is where our fulfillment and identity come from. We know who we are because of Whose we are.

✦ As we look unto Jesus, who endured the cross for us, our veil will be removed so we can behold and reflect the glory of the Lord.

✦ My hope and prayer is that you will fill your heart up with the precious truth of God in His Word who calls you who you are.

✦ Cry out to God in His name(s), then go out to a world that is on the other side of your trials and suffering, just waiting to hear the powerful message God has written on your heart because you trusted God to keep His promises.

Let's Reflect:

1. In Appendix D there are select verses from the book of Psalms with God's "name." Now that you are more conscious of the depth and meaning of His name, meditate on and bless His name in the new light you have. Write a prayer to Him naming Him and praising Him.

2. Take the 30-Day Discovery Challenge. For 30 days (and hopefully beyond), practice the principles you have learned and discover intimacy with the God of the universe who is worthy to behold and of Whose love you are worthy! Each day:

   ✿ Choose a name of God (Jesus) from Appendix B or C that is applicable to the situation you are walking through. Cry out to Him to reveal Himself to you through His name in that trial or joy. Write a prayer of thanksgiving to God for how He seeks relationship with you through His matchless love and attributes in the "classroom" he has allowed in your life.

☆ Choose a verse from Appendix E: Who God Calls You. Reminding yourself who God calls you through the day will transform your thoughts about who you are. Write the verse down and carry it with you, write it on the bathroom mirror or post it on the refrigerator, in the car, or at the office. Meditate on it. Thank Him for who He calls you. Write a prayer of thanks.

3. Share what you have learned on this journey with someone who needs to hear this message. I would love to hear it too! Email me at: drodriguezauthor@gmail.com or see my website authordeborahrodriguez.com

Let's Pray:

Faithful Father, I thank You for your pursuing love. Thank You for revealing who You are through Your matchless name. Thank You for unveiling who we are in Christ Jesus. Thank You for Your presence, peace and purpose. Thank You for Your Son, Jesus Christ, who made it possible to know You intimately. You are good. In Jesus' name, Amen.

Let's Sing:

Sing along with my sister on piano by scanning the QR code or visit my website under "Hymns in My Book."

authordeborahrodriguez.com

APPENDIX A

HELPFUL RESOURCES

- *Boundaries: When to Say Yes, How to Say No to Take Control of Your Life by Dr. Henry Cloud and Dr. John Townsend*
- *Emotionally Healthy Spirituality: It's Impossible to be Spiritually Mature, While Remaining Emotionally Immature by Peter Scazzero*
- *The Emotionally Healthy Woman by Geri Scazzero*
- *Knowing God by Name: Names of God That Bring Hope and Healing by David Wilkerson*
- *Lies Women Believe: And the Truth that Sets Them Free by Nancy DeMoss Wolgemuth*
- *The Prayer of Jabez: Breaking Through to the Blessed Life by Bruce Wilkinson*
- *Fully Alive: Learning to Flourish-Mind, Body and Spirit by Susie Larson*
- *Praying the Names of God by Ann Spangler*
- *Praying the Names of Jesus by Ann Spangler*
- https://www.fathersloveletter.com/media-center.html

APPENDIX B

NAMES OF GOD

I AM THAT I AM—YHWH

"I am the LORD; that is my name! I will not yield my glory to another or my praise to idols" (Isaiah 42:8 NIV).

"When the LORD called Moses from the burning bush telling him to go to Pharaoh and lead His children of Israel out of Egypt, Moses asked, 'Who shall I say sent me?' And the LORD said, 'I AM that I AM, tell them that I AM sent you!'" (Exodus 3:11).

Names of our Heavenly Father

Ab (Abba)—father, Daddy, Psalm 68:5

Adonai—LORD, Master, Genesis 15:2

Ehyeh Asher Ehyeh- I Am that I Am, existed, the eternal, all-sufficient God, Exodus 3:14

El—The word "El" indicates The Great Power of God.

El Bethel—God of the House of God, Genesis 35:7

El Chaiyim—Living God of my Life, Jeremiah 10:10; Psalm 42:2; Deuteronomy 5:26

El De'ot—God of All, Knowledge, I Samuel 2:3

El Elohe Yisrael—Mighty God of Israel, Genesis 33:20

El Elyon—Most High God, Genesis 14:18-20, 22; Daniel 3:26
El Emet—God of Truth, Psalm 31:5; Isaiah 65:16
El Emunah—Faithful God, Deuteronomy 7:9
Elohei Haelohim—God of gods, Deuteronomy 10:17
Elohei Marom—God of Heights, Micah 6:6
Elohe Tishuathi—God of my Salvation, Psalm 51:14
Elohe Tsadeki—God of my Righteousness, Psalm 4:1
Elohe Yakob—God of Jacob, Psalm 20:1
Elohe Ohim—God mighty, strong, Exodus 21:6
Elohim Chaseddi—God of My Mercy, Psalm 59:10
Elohim Tsebaoth—God of Hosts, Psalm 80:7
El Gibhor—Strong and Mighty God, Isaiah 10:21
El HaGadol—Great God, grand, awesome, Deuteronomy 10:17
El HaKadosh—The Holy God, Isaiah 1;4
El HaKavod—Most Glorious God, The God of Glory, Psalm 29:3
El HaNe'eman—The Faithful God, Deuteronomy 7:9
El Hashamayim—God of the Heavens, Nehemiah 1:4-5
El Hayyay—God of my Life, Psalm 4; Jealous God, Exodus 20:5
El Kedem—God of the Beginning, Deuteronomy 33:27
El Mauzi—God of my Strength, Psalm 43:2
El Mishpat—God of Justice, Isaiah 30:18
El Nekamoth—God that Avenges, Psalm 18:47
Elohei Tehillati—God of My Praise, Psalm 109:1
Elohenu Olam—Our Everlasting God, Psalm 48:14
Elohei Chasdi—God of my Kindness, Psalm 59:17
Elohei Ma'uzzi—God of my Strength, 2 Samuel 22:33
Elohei Mikkarov—God Who is Near, Jeremiah 23:23
El Ohim—God Judge, Creator, Genesis 1:1
Elohim Bashamayim—God in Heaven, Joshua 2:11

Elohim Chayim—Living God, Joshua 3:10

Elohim Kedoshim—Holy God, Joshua 24:19

Elohim Machase Lanu—God Our Refuge, Psalm 62:8

Elohim Ozer Li—God my Helper, Psalm 54:4

Elohim Shophtim Ba-arets—God that Judges in the Earth, Psalm 58:11

El Olam—The Everlasting God, Psalm 90:1-2

El Rachum—Merciful God, Deuteronomy 4:31

El Rai—God That Sees Me, Genesis 16:13

El Sali—God My Rock, 2 Samuel 22:47; Psalm 42:9

El Selichot—God of Forgiveness, Nehemiah 9:17

El Shaddai—All-Sufficient, Genesis 17:1

El Simchath Gili—God my Exceeding Joy, Psalm 43:4

El Tehilati—God of my Praise, Psalm 109:1

El Tsadik- Righteous God, Isaiah 45:21

El Tzur—God of Faithfulness, Deuteronomy 32:4

El Yeshuati—God of my Deliverance, Isaiah 12:2

El Yisra'el- God of Israel, Genesis 33:20

Go'el—Kinsman Redeemer, Exodus 15:13

Jehovah—Jehovah is translated as "The Existing One" or "LORD." The chief meaning of Jehovah is derived from the Hebrew word Havah meaning "to be" or "to exist." It also suggests "to become" or specifically "to become known." This denotes a God who reveals Himself unceasingly.

Jehovah Adon Kol Ha-arets—LORD of All the Earth, Joshua 3:11

Jehovah Chereh—the LORD...the Sword, Deuteronomy 33:29

Jehovah El Elohim—LORD God of gods, Mighty, Powerful, Strong One over All, Joshua 22:22

Jehovah El Emeth—LORD God of Truth, Psalm 31:5

Jehovah El Gemuwal—LORD God of Recompense, Jeremiah 51:56

Jehovah Elohim—LORD God, Genesis 2:4

Jehovah Elohim Ab—LORD God of your forefathers, Joshua 18:3

Jehovah Elohim Tsaba—LORD God of Hosts, Psalm 59:5

Jehovah Gibbor Milchamah—LORD Mighty in battle, Psalm 24:8

Jehovah Goelekh—LORD Thy Redeemer, Isaiah 60:16

Jehovah Ha-Melech—LORD the King, Psalm 98:6

Jehovah Hoshiah—O LORD Save, Psalm 20:9

Jehovah Hashopet—LORD the Judge, Judges 11:27

Jehovah Immeka—LORD is with You, Judges 6:12

Jehovah Kanna Shemo—LORD Whose Name is Jealous, Exodus 34:14

Jehovah Jireh—LORD Will Provide: a symbolic name given to Mount Moriah by Abraham to memorialize the intercession of God in the sacrifice of Isaac by providing a substitute for the sacrifice of his son, Genesis 22:14

Jehovah Machsi—LORD my Refuge, Psalm 91:9

Jehovah Magen—LORD my Shield, Deuteronomy 33:29

Jehovah Maginnenu—LORD Our Defense, Psalm 89:18

Jehovah Mauzzi—LORD my Fortress, Jeremiah 16:19

Jehovah Mephalti—LORD my Deliverer, Psalm 18:2

Jehovah Mekoddishkem—LORD Who Sanctifies You, Makes Holy, Exodus 31:33; Leviticus 20:8

Jehovah Metsudhathi—LORD my High Tower, Psalm 18:2

Jehovah Moshiekh—LORD Your Savior, Isaiah 49:26

Jehovah Nissi—LORD my Banner, Exodus 17:15

Jehovah Ori—LORD my Light, Psalm 27:1

Jehovah-Raah—LORD my Shepherd, Psalm 23; Ezekiel 34: 11-15

Jehovah Rapha (Jehovah Rophe)—LORD That Heals, Exodus 15:26; Jeremiah 30;17; 3:22; Isaiah 30:26; 61:1; Psalm 103:3

Jehovah Roi—LORD my Shepherd, Psalm 23:1

Jehovah Sabaoth—LORD of Host, I Samuel 1:3

Jehovah Sal'l—LORD my Rock, Psalm 18:2

Jehovah Shalom—LORD is Peace, Judges 6:24

Jehovah Shammah—LORD is There, Ezekiel 48:35

Jehovah Tsaba—LORD of Hosts, I Samuel 17:45

Jehovah Tsidkenu—LORD Our Rightness, Jeremiah 23:6; 33:16

Kadosh—Holy One, Isaiah 40:25

Or Goyim—Light of the Nations, Isaiah 42:6

Qanna—Jealous, exodus 20:5; 34:14; Deuteronomy 4:24; 5:9

Yahweh—LORD Jehovah, Master, despot, absolute ruler, denoting the omnipotence of God, Genesis 2:4

Used by permission from:

Gospel Tract Society, Inc.

PO Box 1118

Independence, MO 64051

www.gospeltractsociety.org

APPENDIX C

NAMES OF JESUS

The following is from "All the Names of Jesus" written by Betty Miller.

The more we study this list, the more we will understand who Jesus really is. How can we help but love Him?

All Scriptures are taken from the King James Version of the Bible.

ADAM: (1 Corinthians 15:45) And so it is written, The first man Adam was made a living soul; the last Adam was made a quickening spirit.

ADVOCATE: (1 John 2:1) My little children, these things write I unto you, that ye sin not. And if any man sin, we have an advocate with the Father, Jesus Christ the righteous:

ALMIGHTY: (Revelation 1:8) I am Alpha and Omega, the beginning and the ending, saith the Lord, which is, and which was, and which is to come, the Almighty.

ALPHA AND OMEGA: (Revelation 1:8) I am Alpha and Omega, the beginning and the ending, saith the Lord, which is, and which was, and which is to come, the Almighty.

AMEN: (Revelation 3:14) And unto the angel of the church of the Laodiceans write; These things saith the Amen, the faithful and true witness, the beginning of the creation of God;

APOSTLE OF OUR PROFESSION: (Hebrews 3:1) Wherefore, holy brethren, partakers of the heavenly calling, consider the Apostle and High Priest of our profession, Christ Jesus;

ARM OF THE LORD: (Isaiah 51:9) Awake, awake, put on strength, O arm of the LORD; awake, as in the ancient days, in the generations of old. Art thou not it that hath cut Rahab, and wounded the dragon?

(Isaiah 53:1) Who hath believed our report? and to whom is the arm of the LORD revealed?

AUTHOR AND FINISHER OF OUR FAITH: (Hebrews 12:2) Looking unto Jesus the author and finisher of our faith; who for the joy that was set before him endured the cross, despising the shame, and is set down at the right hand of the throne of God.

AUTHOR OF ETERNAL SALVATION: (Hebrews 5:9) And being made perfect, he became the author of eternal salvation unto all them that obey him;

BEGINNING OF CREATION OF GOD: (Revelation 3:14) And unto the angel of the church of the Laodiceans write; These things saith the Amen, the faithful and true witness, the beginning of the creation of God;

BELOVED SON: (Matthew 12:18) Behold my servant, whom I have chosen; my beloved, in whom my soul is well pleased: I will put my spirit upon him, and he shall show judgment to the Gentiles.

BLESSED AND ONLY POTENTATE: (1 Timothy 6:15) Which in his times he shall show, who is the blessed and only Potentate, the King of kings, and Lord of lords;

BRANCH: (Isaiah 4:2) In that day shall the branch of the LORD be beautiful and glorious, and the fruit of the earth shall be excellent and comely for them that are escaped of Israel.

BREAD OF LIFE: (John 6:32) Then Jesus said unto them, Verily, verily, I say unto you, Moses gave you not that bread from heaven; but my Father giveth you the true bread from heaven.

CAPTAIN OF SALVATION: (Hebrews 2:10) For it became him, for whom are all things, and by whom are all things, in bringing many sons unto glory, to make the captain of their salvation perfect through sufferings.

CHIEF SHEPHERD: (1 Peter 5:4) And when the chief Shepherd shall appear, ye shall receive a crown of glory that fadeth not away.

CHRIST OF GOD: (Luke 9:20) He said unto them, But whom say ye that I am? Peter answering said, The Christ of God.

CONSOLATION OF ISRAEL: (Luke 2:25) And, behold, there was a man in Jerusalem, whose name was Simeon; and the same man was just and devout, waiting for the consolation of Israel: and the Holy Ghost was upon him.

CORNERSTONE: (Psalm 118:22) The stone which the builders refused is become the head stone of the corner.

COUNSELOR: (Isaiah 9:6) For unto us a child is born, unto us a son is given: and the government shall be upon his shoulder: and his name shall be called Wonderful, Counselor, The mighty God, The everlasting Father, The Prince of Peace.

CREATOR: (John 1:3) All things were made by him; and without him was not any thing made that was made.

DAYSPRING: (Luke 1:78) Through the tender mercy of our God; whereby the dayspring from on high hath visited us,

DELIVERER: (Romans 11:26) And so all Israel shall be saved: as it is written, There shall come out of Zion the Deliverer, and shall turn away ungodliness from Jacob:

DESIRE OF THE NATIONS: (Haggai 2:7) And I will shake all nations, and the desire of all nations shall come: and I will fill this house with glory, saith the LORD of hosts.

DOOR: (John 10:7) Then said Jesus unto them again, Verily, verily, I say unto you, I am the door of the sheep.

ELECT OF GOD: (Isaiah 42:1) Behold my servant, whom I uphold; mine elect, in whom my soul delighteth; I have put my spirit upon him: he shall bring forth judgment to the Gentiles.

EVERLASTING FATHER: (Isaiah 9:6) For unto us a child is born, unto us a son is given: and the government shall be upon his shoulder: and his name shall be called Wonderful, Counsellor, The mighty God, The everlasting Father, The Prince of Peace.

FAITHFUL WITNESS: (Revelation 1:5) And from Jesus Christ, who is the faithful witness, and the first begotten of the dead, and the prince of the kings of the earth. Unto him that loved us, and washed us from our sins in his own blood,

FIRST AND LAST: (Revelation 1:17) And when I saw him, I fell at his feet as dead. And he laid his right hand upon me, saying unto me, Fear not; I am the first and the last:

FIRST BEGOTTEN: (Revelation 1:5) And from Jesus Christ, who is the faithful witness, and the first begotten of the dead, and the prince of the kings of the earth. Unto him that loved us, and washed us from our sins in his own blood,

FORERUNNER: (Hebrews 6:20) Whither the forerunner is for us entered, even Jesus, made an high priest forever after the order of Melchisedec.

GLORY OF THE LORD: (Isaiah 40:5) And the glory of the LORD shall be revealed, and all flesh shall see it together: for the mouth of the LORD hath spoken it.

GOD: (Isaiah 40:3) The voice of him that crieth in the wilderness, Prepare ye the way of the LORD, make straight in the desert a highway for our God.

GOD BLESSED: (Romans 9:5) Whose are the fathers, and of whom as concerning the flesh Christ came, who is over all, God blessed for ever. Amen.

GOOD SHEPHERD: (John 10:11) I am the good shepherd: the good shepherd giveth his life for the sheep.

GOVERNOR: (Matthew 2:6) And thou Bethlehem, in the land of Juda, art not the least among the princes of Juda: for out of thee shall come a Governor, that shall rule my people Israel.

GREAT HIGH PRIEST: (Hebrews 4:14) Seeing then that we have a great high priest, that is passed into the heavens, Jesus the Son of God, let us hold fast our profession.

HEAD OF THE CHURCH: (Ephesians 1:22) And hath put all things under his feet, and gave him to be the head over all things to the church,

HEIR OF ALL THINGS: (Hebrews 1:2) Hath in these last days spoken unto us by his Son, whom he hath appointed heir of all things, by whom also he made the worlds;

HOLY CHILD: (Acts 4:27) For of a truth against thy holy child Jesus, whom thou hast anointed, both Herod, and Pontius Pilate, with the Gentiles, and the people of Israel, were gathered together,

HOLY ONE: (Acts 3:14) But ye denied the Holy One and the Just, and desired a murderer to be granted unto you;

HOLY ONE OF GOD: (Mark 1:24) Saying, Let us alone; what have we to do with thee, thou Jesus of Nazareth? art thou come to destroy us? I know thee who thou art, the Holy One of God.

HOLY ONE OF ISRAEL: (Isaiah 41:14) Fear not, thou worm Jacob, and ye men of Israel; I will help thee, saith the LORD, and thy redeemer, the Holy One of Israel.

HORN OF SALVATION: (Luke 1:69) And hath raised up an horn of salvation for us in the house of his servant David;

I AM: (John 8:58) Jesus said unto them, Verily, verily, I say unto you, Before Abraham was, I am.

IMAGE OF GOD: (2 Corinthians 4:4) In whom the god of this world hath blinded the minds of them which believe not, lest the light of the glorious gospel of Christ, who is the image of God, should shine unto them.

IMMANUEL: (Isaiah 7:14) Therefore the Lord himself shall give you a sign; Behold, a virgin shall conceive, and bear a son, and shall call his name Immanuel.

JEHOVAH: (Isaiah 26:4) Trust ye in the LORD for ever: for in the LORD JEHOVAH is everlasting strength:

JESUS: (Matthew 1:21) And she shall bring forth a son, and thou shalt call his name JESUS: for he shall save his people from their sins.

JESUS OF NAZARETH: (Matthew 21:11) And the multitude said, This is Jesus the prophet of Nazareth of Galilee.

JUDGE OF ISRAEL: (Micah 5:1) Now gather thyself in troops, O daughter of troops: he hath laid siege against us: they shall smite the judge of Israel with a rod upon the cheek.

THE JUST ONE: (Acts 7:52) Which of the prophets have not your fathers persecuted? and they have slain them which showed before of the coming of the Just One; of whom ye have been now the betrayers and murderers:

KING: (Zechariah 9:9) Rejoice greatly, O daughter of Zion; shout, O daughter of Jerusalem: behold, thy King cometh unto thee: he is just, and having salvation; lowly, and riding upon an ass, and upon a colt the foal of an ass.

KING OF THE AGES: (1 Timothy 1:17) Now unto the King eternal, immortal, invisible, the only wise God, be honor and glory for ever and ever. Amen.

KING OF THE JEWS: (Matthew 2:2) Saying, Where is he that is born King of the Jews? for we have seen his star in the east, and are come to worship him.

KING OF KINGS: (1 Timothy 6:15) Which in his times he shall show, who is the blessed and only Potentate, the King of kings, and Lord of lords;

KING OF SAINTS: (Revelation 15:3) And they sing the song of Moses the servant of God, and the song of the Lamb, saying, Great and marvelous are thy works, Lord God Almighty; just and true are thy ways, thou King of saints.

LAWGIVER: (Isaiah 33:22) For the LORD is our judge, the LORD is our lawgiver, the LORD is our king; he will save us.

LAMB: (Revelation 13:8) And all that dwell upon the earth shall worship him, whose names are not written in the book of life of the Lamb slain from the foundation of the world.

LAMB OF GOD: (John 1:29) The next day John seeth Jesus coming unto him, and saith, Behold the Lamb of God, which taketh away the sin of the world.

LEADER AND COMMANDER: (Isaiah 55:4) Behold, I have given him for a witness to the people, a leader and commander to the people.

THE LIFE: (John 14:6) Jesus saith unto him, I am the way, the truth, and the life: no man cometh unto the Father, but by me.

LIGHT OF THE WORLD: (John 8:12) Then spake Jesus again unto them, saying, I am the light of the world: he that followeth me shall not walk in darkness, but shall have the light of life.

LION OF THE TRIBE OF JUDAH: (Revelation 5:5) And one of the elders saith unto me, Weep not: behold, the Lion of the tribe of Judah, the Root of David, hath prevailed to open the book, and to loose the seven seals thereof.

LORD OF ALL: (Acts 10:36) The word which God sent unto the children of Israel, preaching peace by Jesus Christ: (he is Lord of all:)

LORD OF GLORY: (1 Corinthians 2:8) Which none of the princes of this world knew: for had they known it, they would not have crucified the Lord of glory.

LORD OF LORDS: (1 Timothy 6:15) Which in his times he shall show, who is the blessed and only Potentate, the King of kings, and Lord of lords;

LORD OF OUR RIGHTEOUSNESS: (Jeremiah 23:6) In his days Judah shall be saved, and Israel shall dwell safely: and this is his name whereby he shall be called, THE LORD OUR RIGHTEOUSNESS.

MAN OF SORROWS: (Isaiah 53:3) He is despised and rejected of men; a man of sorrows, and acquainted with grief: and we hid as it were our faces from him; he was despised, and we esteemed him not.

MEDIATOR: (1 Timothy 2:5) For there is one God, and one mediator between God and men, the man Christ Jesus;

MESSENGER OF THE COVENANT: (Malachi 3:1) Behold, I will send my messenger, and he shall prepare the way before me: and the Lord, whom ye seek, shall suddenly come to his temple, even the messenger of the covenant, whom ye delight in: behold, he shall come, saith the LORD of hosts.

MESSIAH: (Daniel 9:25) Know therefore and understand, that from the going forth of the commandment to restore and to build Jerusalem unto the Messiah the Prince shall be seven weeks, and threescore and two weeks: the street shall be built again, and the wall, even in troublous times.

(John 1:41) He first findeth his own brother Simon, and saith unto him, We have found the Messiah, which is, being interpreted, the Christ.

MIGHTY GOD: (Isaiah 9:6) For unto us a child is born, unto us a son is given: and the government shall be upon his shoulder: and his name shall be called Wonderful, Counsellor, The mighty God, The everlasting Father, The Prince of Peace.

MIGHTY ONE: (Isaiah 60:16) Thou shalt also suck the milk of the Gentiles, and shalt suck the breast of kings: and thou shalt know that I the LORD am thy Saviour and thy Redeemer, the mighty One of Jacob.

MORNING STAR: (Revelation 22:16) I Jesus have sent mine angel to testify unto you these things in the churches. I am the root and the offspring of David, and the bright and morning star.

NAZARENE: (Matthew 2:23) And he came and dwelt in a city called Nazareth: that it might be fulfilled which was spoken by the prophets, He shall be called a Nazarene.

ONLY BEGOTTEN SON: (John 1:18) No man hath seen God at any time; the only begotten Son, which is in the bosom of the Father, he hath declared him.

OUR PASSOVER: (1 Corinthians 5:7) Purge out therefore the old leaven, that ye may be a new lump, as ye are unleavened. For even Christ our passover is sacrificed for us:

PRINCE OF LIFE: (Acts 3:15) And killed the Prince of life, whom God hath raised from the dead; whereof we are witnesses.

PRINCE OF KINGS: (Revelation 1:5) And from Jesus Christ, who is the faithful witness, and the first begotten of the dead, and the prince of the kings of the earth. Unto him that loved us, and washed us from our sins in his own blood,

PRINCE OF PEACE: (Isaiah 9:6) For unto us a child is born, unto us a son is given: and the government shall be upon his shoulder: and his name shall be called Wonderful, Counsellor, The mighty God, The everlasting Father, The Prince of Peace.

PROPHET: (Luke 24:19) And he said unto them, What things? And they said unto him, Concerning Jesus of Nazareth, which was a prophet mighty in deed and word before God and all the people:

(Acts 3:22) For Moses truly said unto the fathers, A prophet shall the Lord your God raise up unto you of your brethren, like unto me; him shall ye hear in all things whatsoever he shall say unto you.

REDEEMER: (Job 19:25) For I know that my redeemer liveth, and that he shall stand at the latter day upon the earth:

RESURRECTION AND LIFE: (John 11:25) Jesus said unto her, I am the resurrection, and the life: he that believeth in me, though he were dead, yet shall he live.

ROCK: (1 Corinthians 10:4) And did all drink the same spiritual drink: for they drank of that spiritual Rock that followed them: and that Rock was Christ.

ROOT OF DAVID: (Revelation 22:16) I Jesus have sent mine angel to testify unto you these things in the churches. I am the root and the offspring of David, and the bright and morning star.

ROSE OF SHARON: (Song of Songs 2:1) I am the rose of Sharon, and the lily of the valleys.

SAVIOR: (Luke 2:11) For unto you is born this day in the city of David a Saviour, which is Christ the Lord.

SEED OF WOMAN: (Genesis 3:15) And I will put enmity between thee and the woman, and between thy seed and her seed; it shall bruise thy head, and thou shalt bruise his heel.

SHEPHERD AND BISHOP OF SOULS: (1 Peter 2:25) For ye were as sheep going astray; but are now returned unto the Shepherd and Bishop of your souls.

SHILOH: (Genesis 49:10) The scepter shall not depart from Judah, nor a lawgiver from between his feet, until Shiloh come; and unto him shall the gathering of the people be.

SON OF THE BLESSED: (Mark 14:61) But he held his peace, and answered nothing. Again the high priest asked him, and said unto him, Art thou the Christ, the Son of the Blessed?

SON OF DAVID: (Matthew 1:1) The book of the generation of Jesus Christ, the son of David, the son of Abraham.

SON OF GOD: (Matthew 2:15) And was there until the death of Herod: that it might be fulfilled which was spoken of the Lord by the prophet, saying, Out of Egypt have I called my son.

SON OF THE HIGHEST: (Luke 1:32) He shall be great, and shall be called the Son of the Highest: and the Lord God shall give unto him the throne of his father David:

SUN OF RIGHTEOUSNESS: (Malachi 4:2) But unto you that fear my name shall the Sun of righteousness arise with healing in his wings; and ye shall go forth, and grow up as calves of the stall.

TRUE LIGHT: (John 1:9) That was the true Light, which lighteth every man that cometh into the world.

TRUE VINE: (John 15:1) I am the true vine, and my Father is the husbandman.

TRUTH: (John 1:14) And the Word was made flesh, and dwelt among us, (and we beheld his glory, the glory as of the only begotten of the Father,) full of grace and truth.

WITNESS: (Isaiah 55:4) Behold, I have given him for a witness to the people, a leader and commander to the people.

WORD: (John 1:1) In the beginning was the Word, and the Word was with God, and the Word was God.

WORD OF GOD: (Revelation 19:13) And he was clothed with a vesture dipped in blood: and his name is called The Word of God.

Used with permission:

by Betty Miller, Copyright ©2013 by Christ Unlimited Ministries/BibleResources.org

APPENDIX D

SELECT VERSES IN THE PSALMS WITH THE WORD "NAME"

Prepare to adore God's name by inserting a name of God (Jesus) as you meditate on these verses. For example: *"For our heart shall rejoice in Him, Because we have trusted in His holy name (Jehovah Rapha- God Who Heals)"* (Psalm 33:21).

1. *"But let all those rejoice who put their trust in You, Let them ever shout for joy, because You defend them, Let those also who love Your name Be joyful in You"* (Psalm 5:11).
2. *"I will praise the LORD according to His righteousness, And will sing praise to the name of the LORD Most High"* (Psalm 7:17).
3. *"O LORD, our Lord, How excellent is Your name in all the earth!"* (Psalm 8:9).
4. *"I will be glad and rejoice in You; I will sing praise to Your name, O Most High"* (Psalm 9:2).
5. *"And those who know Your name will put their trust in You; For You, LORD, have not forsaken those who seek You"* (Psalm 9:10).

6. *"Therefore I will give thanks to You, O LORD, among the Gentiles, And sing praises to Your name"* (Psalm 18:49).

7. *"May the LORD answer you in the day of trouble; May the name of the God of Jacob defend you"* (Psalm 20:1).

8. *"We will rejoice in your salvation, And in the name of our God we will set up our banners! May the LORD fulfill all your petitions"* (Psalm 20:5).

9. *"Some trust in chariots, and some in horses; But we will remember the name of the LORD our God"* (Psalm 20:7).

10. *"I will declare Your name to My brethren; In the midst of the assembly I will praise You"* (Psalm 22:22).

11. *"Give unto the LORD the glory due to His name; Worship the LORD in the beauty of holiness"* (Psalm 29:2).

12. *"Sing praise to the LORD, you saints of His, And give thanks at the remembrance of His holy name"* (Psalm 30:4).

13. *"For our heart shall rejoice in Him, Because we have trusted in His holy name"* (Psalm 33:21).

14. *"Oh, magnify the LORD with me, And let us exalt His name together"* (Psalm 34:3).

15. *"Through You we will push down our enemies; Through Your name we will trample those who rise up against us"* (Psalm 44:5).

16. *"In God we boast all day long, And praise Your name forever. Selah"* (Psalm 44:8."

17. *"According to your name, O God, So is Your praise to the ends of the earth, Your right hand is full of righteousness"* (Psalm 48:10).

18. *"I will praise You forever, Because You have done it; And in the presence of Your saints I will wait on Your name, for it is good"* (Psalm 52:9).

19. *"Save me, O God, by your name, And vindicate me by Your strength"* (Psalm 54:1).

20. *"I will freely sacrifice to You, I will praise Your name, O LORD, for it is good"* (Psalm 54:6).

21. *"For You, O God, have heard my vows; You have given me the heritage of those who fear Your name"* (Psalm 61:5).

22. 22. *"So I will sing praise to Your name forever, That I may daily perform my vows"* (Psalm 61:8).

23. *"Thus I will bless You while I live; I will lift up my hands in Your name"* (Psalm 63:4).

24. *"Sing out the honor of His name; Make His praise glorious"* (Psalm 66:2).

25. *"Sing to God, sing praises to His name; Extol Him who rides on the clouds, By His name YAH, And rejoice before Him"* (Psalm 68:4).

26. *"I will praise the name of God with a song, And will magnify Him with thanksgiving"* (Psalm 69:30).

27. *"His name shall endure forever; His name shall continue as long as the sun. And men shall be blessed in Him; All nations shall call Him blessed"* (Psalm 72:17).

28. *"And blessed be His glorious name forever! And let the whole earth be filled with His glory. Amen and Amen"* (Psalm 72:19).

29. *"We give thanks to You, O God, we give thanks! For Your wondrous works declare that Your name is near"* (Psalm 75:1).

30. *"Help us, O God of our salvation, For the glory of Your name; And deliver us, and provide atonement for our sins, For Your name's sake!"* (Psalm 79:9).

31. *"Then we will not turn back from You, Revive us, and we will call upon Your name"* (Psalm 80:18).

32. *"That they may know that You, whose name alone is the LORD, Are the Most High over all the earth"* (Psalm 83:18).

33. *"All nations whom You have made Shall come and worship before You, O Lord, And shall glorify Your name"* (Psalm 86:9).

34. *"Teach me Your way, O LORD; I will walk in Your truth; Unite my heart to fear Your name"* (Psalm 86:11).

35. *"I will praise You, O Lord my God, with all my heart, And I will glorify Your name forevermore"* (Psalm 86:12).

36. *"Because he has set his love upon Me, therefore I will deliver him; I will set him on high, because he has known My name"* (Psalm 91:14).

37. *"It is good to give thanks to the LORD, And to sing praises to Your name, O Most High"* (Psalm 92:1).

38. *"Sing to the LORD, bless His name; Proclaim the good news of His salvation from day to day"* (Psalm 96:2).

39. *"Rejoice in the LORD, you righteous, And give thanks at the remembrance of His holy name"* (Psalm 97:12).

40. *"Enter into His gates with thanksgiving, And into His courts with praise. Be thankful to Him, and bless His name"* (Psalm 100:4).

41. *"Bless the LORD, O my soul; And all that is within me, bless His holy name!"* (Psalm 103:1).

42. *"Oh, give thanks to the LORD! Call upon His name; Make known His deeds among the peoples!"* (Psalm 105:1).

43. *"Glory in His holy name: Let the hearts of those rejoice who seek the LORD!"* (Psalm 105:3).

44. *"He has sent redemption to His people; He has commanded His covenant forever: Holy and awesome is His name"* (Psalm 111:9).

45. *"Praise the LORD! Praise, O servants of the LORD, Praise the name of the LORD! Blessed be the name of the LORD From this time forth and forevermore! From the rising of the sun to its going down The LORD's name is to be praised"* (Psalm 113:1-3).

46. *"Not unto us, O LORD, not unto us, But to Your name give glory, Because of Your mercy, Because of Your truth"* (Psalm 115:1).

47. *"Then I called upon the name of the LORD: "O LORD, I implore You, deliver my soul!"* (Psalm 116:4).

48. *"I will offer to You the sacrifice of thanksgiving, And will call upon the name of the LORD"* (Psalm 116:17).

49. *"Blessed is he who comes in the name of the LORD! We have blessed you from the house of the LORD"* (Psalm 118:26).

50. *"I remember Your name in the night, O LORD, And I keep Your law"* (Psalm 119:55).

51. "Look upon me and be merciful to me, As Your custom is toward those who love Your name" (Psalm 119:132)

52. *"Our help is in the name of the LORD, Who made heaven and earth"* (Psalm 124:8).

53. *"Praise the LORD, for the LORD is good; Sing praises to His name, for it is pleasant"* (Psalm 135:3).

54. *"Your name, O LORD, endures forever, Your fame, O LORD, throughout all generations"* (Psalm 135:13).

55. *"I will worship toward Your holy temple, And praise Your name For Your lovingkindness and Your truth; For You have magnified Your word above all Your name"* (Psalm 138:2).

56. *"Surely the righteous shall give thanks to Your name; The upright shall dwell in Your presence"* (Psalm 140:13).

57. *"Bring my soul out of prison, That I may praise Your name; The righteous shall surround me, For You shall deal bountifully with me"* (Psalm 142:7).

58. *"I will extol You, my God, O King; And I will bless Your name forever and ever"* (Psalm 145:1).

59. *"Every day I will bless You, And I will praise Your name forever and ever"* (Psalm 145:2).

60. *"My mouth shall speak the praise of the LORD, And all flesh shall bless His holy name Forever and ever"* (Psalm 145:21).

APPENDIX E

WHO GOD CALLS YOU

I am a child of God. (John 1:12, I John 3:1)

I am an heir of God and joint-heir with Christ. (Romans 8:16-17)

I am God's workmanship... I am created in Christ Jesus to do good works. (Ephesians 2:10)

I am forgiven. (Ephesians 1:7)

I am blessed with every spiritual blessing in the heavenly places in Christ. (Ephesians 1:3)

I am complete in Him. (Colossians 2:10)

I am free from condemnation. (Romans 8:1)

I am delivered from the power of darkness and conveyed into the kingdom of the Son of His love in whom I have redemption through His blood, the forgiveness of sins. (Colossians 1:13-14)

I am the temple of God and that the Spirit of God dwells in me. (I Corinthians 3:16)

I am loved with God's great love... I am alive with Christ... I am sitting in heavenly places in Christ Jesus. (Ephesians 2:4-6)

I am rejoiced over with gladness, I am quieted with His love, I am rejoiced over with singing. (Zephaniah 3:17)

I am a new creation; old things have passed away; ... all things have become new. (2 Corinthians 5:17)

I am fearfully and wonderfully made; I am a marvelous work. (Psalm 139:14)

I am someone that the wicked one does not touch. (I John 5:18)

I am the apple of God's eye. (Psalm 17:8)

I am being transformed into Christ's image with ever-increasing glory, which comes from the Lord. (2 Corinthians 3:18)

I am the head and not the tail; I am above only, and not beneath if I heed the commandments of the Lord my God. (Deuteronomy 28:13)

I am rescued from the dominion of darkness and brought into the kingdom of the Son God loves. (Colossians 1:13)

I am never left alone or forsaken. (Deuteronomy 31:8)

I am a chosen generation, a royal priesthood, a holy nation, His own special people, that I may proclaim the praises of Him who called me out of darkness into His marvelous light. (I Peter 2:9-10)

I am victorious through our Lord Jesus Christ. (I Corinthians 15:57)

I am loved with an everlasting love. (Jeremiah 31:3)

I am more than a conqueror through Christ who loved me. (Romans 8:37)

I am no longer a slave, but God's child; and since I am his child, God has made me also an heir. (Galatians 4:7)

I am redeemed and need not fear... I am summoned by my name and I am His... I am not abandoned when I pass through the waters, or when I walk through the fire for God is with me... I am precious and honored in His sight because He loves me. (Isaiah 43:1-4)

I am a special treasure to God if I obey His voice and keep His covenant. (Exodus 19:5)

I am provided for all my needs according to God's riches in glory by Christ Jesus. (Philippians 4:19)

I am clothed with garments of salvation and arrayed in a robe of his righteousness as a bride adorns herself with her jewels. (Isaiah 61:10)

I am rejoiced over just as a bridegroom rejoices over his bride. (Isaiah 62:5)

I am Jesus Christ's friend. (John 15:15)

I am strong in the Lord and in the power of His might. (Ephesians 6:10)

I am given a spirit of power and of love and of a sound mind. (2 Timothy 1.7)

I am a partaker of the divine nature, having escaped the corruption *that is* in the world through lust. (2 Peter 1:4)

I am confident of this very thing, that He who has begun a good work in me will complete *it* until the day of Jesus Christ. (Philippians 1:6)

I am washed, sanctified, and justified in the name of the Lord Jesus and by the Spirit of our God. (I Corinthians 6:11)

I am created in God's own image. (Genesis 1:27)

I am strong when I am weak because God said, "My grace is sufficient for you, for My strength is made perfect in weakness." (2 Corinthians 12:9-11)

I am a new creation when I am in Christ... old things have passed away; behold all things have become new. (2 Corinthians 5:17)

I am justified freely by His grace through the redemption that is in Christ Jesus. (Romans 3:23-25)

I am redeemed and forgiven of my sins through Christ's blood according to the riches of His grace. (Ephesians 1:7)

I am more than a conqueror through Christ who loved me. (Romans 8:37)

I am crucified with Christ... and the life which I now live in the flesh I live by faith in the Son of God, who loved me and gave Himself for me. (Galatians 2:20)

I am able to do all things through Christ who strengthens me. (Philippians 4:13)

I am assured that all things work together for good to those who love God, to those who are called according to His purpose. (Romans 8:28)

I am an overcomer by the blood of the Lamb and by the word of my testimony. (Revelation 12:10-11)

I am indeed Christ's disciple if I abide in His Word. (John 8:31)

I am healed by Christ's wounds. (1 Peter 2:24)

I am a son/daughter of God through faith in Christ Jesus. (Galatians 3:26)

I am continually being worked in, to will, and to act in order to fulfill God's good purpose. (Philippians 2:13)

APPENDIX F

RECEIVING THE GIFT OF SALVATION

What a wonder! Christ redeems us that we might receive His adoption as His child. As His child, an heir of God, we can cry out to Him, "Daddy!" We are heirs to the King of the universe through Jesus Christ! We are royalty! *"You are a chosen generation, a royal priesthood, a holy nation, His own special people, that you may proclaim the praises of Him who called you out of darkness into His marvelous light"* (I Peter 2:9).

But...

We can only claim these promises of blessing and reward as we experientially and intimately know our Lord and Savior Jesus Christ. *"But without faith it is impossible to please Him, for he who comes to God must believe that He is, and that He is a rewarder of those who diligently seek Him"* (Hebrews 11:6). Having peace with God through a loving relationship with Jesus Christ is the greatest gift of all. Have you received the gift of eternal life?

God is El Ha Kadosh (The Holy God). He is Jehovah Mekoddishkem (Lord Who Sanctifies You, Makes you Holy). He is immovable in that He does not overlook sin, yet He pursues you out of His love. Do you desire to run your own life? Obey your own rules? Satisfying the desires of your own sinful flesh breaks His heart and will take you to eternal damnation. He loves you, pursues you, and He gave His life for you.

Can you grasp His pursuing love? Before we even knew Him or understood Him, He valued us and gave His life for us to be free from the bondage of sin. The only way we can genuinely love Jesus is to come to terms with the fact that He first loved and valued us: *"We love Him because He first loved us"* (I John 4:19). One of the first Bible verses we learn in church is John 3:16: *"For God so loved the world that He gave His only begotten Son, that whoever believes in Him should not perish but have everlasting life."* Verse 17 says, *"For God did not send His Son into the world to condemn the world, but that the world through Him might be saved."* He made a way, so we wouldn't have to be condemned eternally, but have everlasting life! Why would we reject Him?

After the "dam of love" broke through that day in my dad's garage, it disrupted thinking that was out of balance. Just as the water crashes into buildings, homes, vegetation, and power lines when there is a dam break, God's love crashed into my heart to clear the debris of unbalanced thinking. Maybe you have thoughts about Jesus that are not true, or out of balance. To *know* Him is to love Him. To love Him is to be compelled to obey Him. I implore you to seek Truth. He has revealed Himself to us by what He did on the cross. *"You see, at just the right time, when we were still powerless, Christ died for the ungodly... But God demonstrates His own love for us in this: While we were still sinners, Christ died for us. Since we have now been justified by his blood, how much more shall we be saved from God's wrath through Him!"* (Romans 5:6,8 NIV).

What is your response? We can surrender to the Holy God of the universe who loves and values us unconditionally, or we can submit to our own desires, self-centeredness, and self-destruction. True belief in Christ Jesus is not just head knowledge. It is unabandoned trust, dependence, and faith in Him that cleanses our heart of sin and self-centeredness, then to walk in His Spirit. The promises of reward and blessing are for those who surrender to Him and choose His ways recorded in His love letter—The Holy Bible.

None of us are good enough to go to heaven because heaven is where God dwells, and He is sinless. We always come short no matter how much good we do. We need to admit we are a sinner and have broken God's commands. *"For all have sinned and fall short of the glory of God"* (Romans 3:23).

Unless we turn away from our life of sin and our self-righteousness, the penalty for our sin is eternal death in a place called Hell. *"For the wages of sin is death, but the gift of God is eternal life in Christ Jesus our Lord"* (Romans 6:23). But the good news is that if we believe with all our heart that Jesus Christ died, was buried, and rose again out of His pursuing love, He will rescue us from eternal separation from Him, *"That if you confess with your mouth the Lord Jesus and believe in your heart that God has raised Him from the dead, you will be saved"* (Romans 10:9).

The Gift of Eternal life is a Gift that was purchased by the blood of Jesus and offered freely to those who call on Him by faith. *"For whoever calls on the name of the LORD shall be saved"* (Romans 10:13).

Will you ask Him today to be your Lord and Savior?

ACKNOWLEDGMENTS

To my parents, who dedicated me to the Lord Jesus Christ when I was conceived and were models of truth and mercy. If I had a hundred lives to live, I could never express my gratitude enough for them pointing me to Jesus Christ and His Word.

To my husband and 6 children who held the fort down at home while I was taking care of Dad. I will probably never know the entirety of your sacrifice to free me up to bless my dad. Washing dishes, laundry, meals, keeping track of needs of younger brothers and sisters, buying groceries, keeping schedules, etc., without me was nothing short of a miracle. Thank you from the bottom of my heart. (P.S. Many nights were spent in tears because I truly missed you.)

To my family, my sister Ruth and her family, and friends, who sacrificed and supported me as God etched His message in my heart during the months following my dad's stroke. Because of your prayers, inspiration, encouragement, service, and admonishment, I have been transformed through the power of the cross. With gratefulness, eternity will reveal the fruit of the investment you made in my life.

To Vanessa Bourne, Elaine Roughton, and Delores Leisner for your experience and insight in editing my book. I learned so much from all of you! You were so patient and kind.

To my sister, Ruth Hartunian-Alumbaugh, for your technology knowledge that is far beyond mine and your musical talent expressed at the end of each chapter brought more beauty to the story God wrote on my heart. With an indebted spirit, I couldn't have impacted lives through this book without you.

To Laura Domino, my hero! We were a match made in heaven when I searched for an accountability partner as a new author. Your experience as an accomplished author, encouragement, prayers and kind spirit propelled me to keep on keeping on. I am forever thankful for you!

To many others who have prayed for me and cheered me on in the author journey. You know who you are! The fruit of your support has been and will be abundant.

To my Lord and Savior Jesus Christ for pursuing me, loving me, revealing who He is to me, and unveiling my identity as His royal child. Thank you for being my Jehovah-Jireh—The Lord My Provider, physically, mentally, emotionally, and spiritually. I'm looking forward to the day when my faith becomes sight and I will know You in Your fullness. You are altogether worthy!

ABOUT THE AUTHOR

From a young age, Deborah had a passion to reach out to those in need. Consequently, she pursued a career as a registered nurse and married a man who surprisingly became the pastor of the church she grew up in. Over the 26 years as a pastor's wife, Deborah was honored to serve the Lord as volunteer coordinator and server for numerous community outreach events, led in women's and children's ministry and joyfully served in various capacities in her small conservative church. As a home-educator, she founded and led a local homeschool support group and has served as a teacher at various homeschool co-ops locally. One of her fulfilled dreams has been to care for her aging parents. Most of all, her greatest earthly treasures are her faithful husband, six precious children, a wonderful son in-law and two special grandsons who bring tremendous joy.

Other books by Deborah Rodriguez (Contributor to a collaboration of 20 women):

Once Upon a Time...God Was Faithful
Amazon Best Seller

If you want to connect with me, I would love to connect with you.
Reach me at email: drodriguezauthor@gmail.com
Facebook: Author Deborah L. Rodriguez or http://bit.ly/45Y0JKv
website: authordeborahrodriguez.com

THANK YOU FOR READING MY BOOK!

CAN YOU HELP ME?

I would really appreciate your feedback, and would love hearing what you have to say.

Please leave me an honest, quick review and rating on Amazon or wherever you purchased this book. Let me know what impacted your life through reading my story. Your review helps to get the message of my book out to those who need it the most. Go to https://www.amazon.com/, search for the name of my book, *Unveiled Identity: From Insignificance to Embracing Your Royal Identity in Christ,* and scroll down to where reviews and ratings are.

With a grateful heart,
Deborah L. Rodriguez

NOW IT'S YOUR TURN!

After sharing some of the life principles God has developed in my life to my Sunday School class, it was enthusiastically conveyed that I should write a book. Their comment struck me like a lightning bolt. Feeling overwhelmed, I slumped into my chair and quietly but audibly said, "Wow." It was the third time in five years that someone told me I should write a book. I immediately remembered telling a friend about three years before that something was keeping me from writing a book, almost as if the kingdom of darkness prevented me. I sensed God saying, "Deborah, it's really Me telling you to do this." It was unmistakably a charge from God! That night I responded, "God, I do not see myself qualified to be an author in the least bit, but I will do it out of sheer obedience." The following day I was scrolling through my Facebook feed, and an advertisement for how to write a faith-based book through Self-Publishing appeared. I had not done any research on writing a book prior to this. God's provision is available for what God calls us to do! The joys and the challenges of self publishing a book has been a life-changing experience. I'm so thankful for this transformational journey!

If you have a passion to share your message to impact the world, consider Self-Publishing. They will give you the tools and experience you need to write your book. You won't be disappointed! Go here for a free resource:

selfpublishing.com/friend/

BIBLIOGRAPHY

Cloud, Henry, and Townsend, John. *Boundaries. Zondervan, 2004.*

Gospel Tract Society, *I Am that I Am: YHWH*

https://www.biblestudytools.com/dictionary/jabez/

Larson, Susie. *Your Sacred Yes.* Bethany House Publishers, 2015.

Scazzero, G. and Scazzero, P. *The Emotionally Healthy Woman.* Zondervan, 2013.

"selfish." Merriam-Webster.com. 2019. https://merriam-webster.com (29 Oct 2019)

"stewardship." Merriam-Webster.com. 2019. https://merriam-webster.com (28 Oct 2019)

Wilkinson, Bruce. *The Prayer of Jabez: Breaking Through to the Blessed Life.* Multnomah Publishers, Inc., 2000.

Wilkinson, Bruce. *30 Days to Discovering Personal Victory Through Holiness.* Multnomah Publishers, Inc., 2003.